Elements

of a SUCCESSFUL
THERAPEUTIC BUSINESS

Robyn Scherr
Kate Mackinnon

ISBN: 978-1-54397-223-8 (print)
ISBN: 978-1-54397-224-5 (ebook)

CONTENTS

INTRODUCTION

Is everything in your business exactly the way you want it?

A healthy, thriving business lives in a state of flux. Change is the constant—we can always think of at least one aspect of our business that could use fine tuning. Whether you are just setting up your therapeutic business or have been practicing for decades, it is helpful to take a fresh look at your business needs and interests.

We are delighted that you have our book in your hands. This is a focused exploration of the elements that we found are most important for the success of our businesses. If you are like us, then you do not want to spend the bulk of your time on business details. You want to be seeing clients who benefit from your work, you want your business to support the meaningful connections you have with your clients, and you want your time away from clients to be truly free.

In the nearly 20 years that we have each been in private practice, we have gotten to know scores of colleagues, and we often talk with them about their work. What we have witnessed is that people can be very gifted and skilled in the therapies they practice, and yet they struggle to develop their businesses. Even practitioners with decades of experience find that they cannot rely on their private practice to be a sustainable source of income and satisfaction.

We see business and therapeutic practice as individual parts of a whole, working together to provide an invaluable resource for clients and a sustainable income for you. After all, the biggest resource for your clients is *you*, so it is essential that you are well supported. Likewise, we view our colleagues as a network of support and not as rivals. Their offices may be nearby to ours, but we do not see them as competition. Rather, we can uplift and develop each other. This concept of mutual support has been essential to each of our individual successes.

We have a strong passion for the work we do, and we know that it is vital for the health of our field to have our colleagues be successful as well. We want as many people as possible to have access to highly effective therapy, and that means having plenty of successful, highly skilled therapists to serve them.

With all this in mind, we sat down and had a long conversation at Kate's kitchen table. What was it exactly that made our business run smoothly? What made our client lists full to the brim and allowed us to sleep at night even if we had a slow week, or knew our practices had to change to make room for something new? What were the elements that made our businesses successful?

We were happy to discover that the same habits we used to build our clinical skills were the habits we used to build our businesses: focused attention applied to what we were working on, consistency in applying the skills we learned, a good deal of compassion, a light-hearted approach, and accountability for our results.

We also discovered that our treatment paradigm as CranioSacral therapy (CST) practitioners fit perfectly with the systems we put in place for our businesses. Business needs attention and time spent skill-building—just like our therapeutic skillset. We both built our businesses with the same focus on integrity and the same precise yet gentle approach that we employ in our therapeutic work.

When we realized the value of business building from a therapeutic mindset, we created an online business class for our colleagues: *Elements of a Successful Craniosacral Business*. We presented what we have learned, and brought in experts we had studied with over the years. Our students were enthusiastic—and those who engaged with the material created inspiring results. They told their friends and colleagues, and we continued to receive requests for our material long after we stopped teaching.

We provided our students a clear and individualized framework to identify, track, and meet their business goals. We also demonstrated how our own quirks and our very individual likes and dislikes are vital cues for how best to build our businesses. Our approach allowed us to bring a lot of fun into the process, because in each class we got to embrace our students' wide panoply of personal styles. And we knew that if we could make business-building fun and a bit of a game, we were all much more likely to stick around to see things through.

We taught hundreds of our colleagues, identifying and addressing the most common issues that challenge practitioners. What we share here comes from our direct experiences as clinicians in solo practice—as well as our students' experiences—reflecting on what worked and what did not. We share our missteps as well as our gems.

Therapeutic work is not like any other business. Often the issues that hinder practitioners' success are tied directly to the containers they hold: both the therapeutic container, and what we came to call the *Business Container*. Our online class was based on our clinical skills and discernment. We applied our clinical skills to our business issues, and we encouraged our students to do the same.

We now want to inspire *you* to bring the clinical discernment, passion, and critical thinking you use in your practice to bear on your business. We provide a solid framework for you to reach the goals you set for yourself. You will have the tools to map your own unique path to success—as you define it.

While many of the concepts in this book can easily apply to businesses with employees and those that are not therapeutic in nature, our focus is on the success of therapeutic practitioners in private practice. Common business wisdom states that we must "scale up" to truly succeed, and that solo practice is a starting place but not a place to remain. Business experts advised us that we must "become bigger" to live well. They advised us to hire employees, start a clinic and then expand to satellite sites, and so on.

But we have discovered that being a solo practitioner is a perfect fit for each of us. Our private practices have become the cornerstones of our businesses, providing the income we need for the lifestyle we want. They are dependable too, which allows us to take on projects that inspire and fulfill us.

We are free to create productive and sincere connections with our clients because our business details are clearly handled. We embrace our personal styles in business, so we have a magnetic quality that pulls in clients who are a good fit for our work. Our hearts and our heads are aligned in our businesses, so we feel whole.

We have a hard time with formulaic approaches to business (and just about everything else), and we know we are not alone in this. Those of us in therapeutic work tend to have a strong non-conformist streak and high levels of creativity. What you will find here is an invitation to delve deeply into who you are in your heart of hearts: why you do what you do, who you are meant to serve and how to inspire them, and what makes you unique in your work. You will find that following our *Business Paradigm* will take you on a courageous journey of discovering yourself in deeper ways while at the same time growing your business. It is a win-win!

We wrote this book so you can shine and succeed, exactly for who you are. Focusing on your unique needs and strengths is in fact what we consider the key to success. We hope the material in this book provides you with inspiration and support to build your own solid foundation in private practice. You can thereafter use that foundation as a springboard to whatever it is that you dream to build.

The business approach we describe here, based on our therapeutic principles, can be applied by all of our colleagues in allied therapies and occupations. Our fellow manual therapists, such as occupational therapists, physical therapists, and massage therapists are a natural fit for our approach. Acupuncturists, energy workers, hair stylists and estheticians, personal trainers and movement instructors have also successfully used our approach. Those who see clients in person as well as those who work remotely will benefit. All that is required is dedication to your own and your clients' growth and self-awareness, and that you are in private practice.

HOW TO USE THIS BOOK

This book has been structured to be read from start to finish. We lay down foundational concepts early on that run throughout every chapter, so even if you feel you have certain topics handled, we suggest you work through the entire book from the beginning.

Our intention is for you to use this book to spark a process of self-discovery, and then apply what you discover to your business practices. With that in mind, we have created a list of questions at the end of each chapter for you work through with a journal. Actively engaging with the material that these questions address is vital for creating the business you want.

We built our businesses with the support of colleagues, and firmly believe that a community of practitioners working together is a powerful force for individual success and the health of our clients. So we encourage you to form a group of like-minded practitioners in your local area. Please share ideas and support one another in problem-solving through the inevitable barriers that surface. One way to build a community is to form a book group. You could review a chapter at each meeting, and perhaps set individual goals that members are willing to be accountable for the next time you get together. Let's lift each other up!

CHAPTER 1

A THERAPEUTIC APPROACH TO BUSINESS

In this chapter, we will explore being present with your business as it is in this moment. You will begin to see what makes your therapeutic business unique (not the therapy that you practice, but the business itself), and you will start to identify how your business can meet the needs of your clients while satisfying your needs as a practitioner. We also explain our Business Paradigm, how to set goals, ways to hold accountability, and how to use your sensations as a reliable guide. These are the foundational components of our approach to business building.

While there are many business-building programs in the world, they tend to follow someone's formula of what is best for everyone, as if there is a right and wrong way to achieve success. We believe that the best way to build your business will be unique to you, which is tailored to your circumstances, preferences, and needs. We provide you with a framework of what we have found to be most effective. We also encourage you to try ideas from other classes and from your colleagues. Then we suggest that you only keep what fits you!

In our online class, it was wonderful to see the wide variety of approaches to building, growing, and evolving successful businesses. When you are acting in accord with your values and the ethical standards of your profession, there is no wrong way to go, but there is a right way for you right now. This is what we are hoping that you will find for yourself as you work through this book.

We practice CranioSacral therapy (CST), and one of the primary tenets of CST is that there is no set protocol for diagnoses or conditions. We treat our clients in the moment, as they show up, and the treatment "plan" evolves organically during the session. This treatment model demands that we stay aware and respond to our client's needs as they arise.

Just like a CST session, the ways we craft our businesses have to be unique to our circumstances, to the ways we are wired, to our preferences, and to our needs. These aspects of ourselves also change over time, so it is vital that we do not simply set a plan and then run on autopilot. This may require more work at first because you will need to engage in your own self-discovery to realize what you want to create. We think that this investment is time well spent, as it guides you to create a business that you will love—one that will fit you like a glove!

FOUNDATIONAL QUESTIONS TO GUIDE YOUR PROCESS

Too many of us start our businesses, or decide we need to make radical changes to our businesses, without adequate information. We need to define just what it is that we really want or we may not be able to recognize what we need to do to achieve it or recognize when we have indeed achieved it. We also need to know where we are today, so that we can chart a course toward where we want to be. It is much easier to plan a trip to your destination when you know your starting place.

What Does a Successful Business Mean to You?

Please take some time to think about this. What is success to you today? Is it making a living seeing clients? Or is that piece covered for you and your intention is to seek new challenges?

If you are at the very beginning of building your business and your idea of a successful business is a six figure income or having a wellness center with likeminded practitioners, we ask that you bring yourself a little closer to the present moment: what would success mean to you today, in a month, and in the next three months? We know grand plans are exciting and can be a wonderful North Star to guide us, but there are many milestones along the way to recognize and celebrate, and skipping them can mean the difference between achieving our dreams and just having dreams.

We still continue to ask ourselves, "What does success mean to me *today*" because we recognize that our answers to that question have changed several times over the past two decades as solo practitioners.

At first, success meant just seeing paying clients—any paying clients at all—as we worked on our clinical skills and continued our education in the classroom and in study groups. Other jobs paid the bulk of our bills. Kate was working as a Physical Therapist for the California Children's Service and Robyn was the publications manager at a consulting firm. As our client load increased (and our income increased along with it), we had to cut down to part time at our jobs. Then, at some point, we each took the plunge, left our steady jobs, and relied on our bodywork businesses to support us fully (more on this in Chapter 4).

Over time, our interests evolved and our businesses had to evolve too. We needed to carve out time for something new. We each still make the bulk of our income from private practice by seeing clients one-on-one in our offices. But our income grew to where we could take out time to engage in other pursuits—working as a team in multihands sessions , writing books and articles, and teaching. Not all of these pursuits are high-paying, nor did we intend them to be! But they do feed us, engage us in developing our skills, and serve our mission of bringing the therapy we practice further out into the world. And truthfully, some of them have, in fact, turned out to be quite lucrative.

How Our Businesses Look Today

Robyn sees between 16 and 24 clients a week. She teaches classes a few times a year either in person or online, mentors about a dozen CST therapists, promotes the adoption of nonintrusive touch and CST in healthcare settings, writes articles for trade magazines, and is often interviewed for podcasts and articles. She also edited Kate's book on CranioSacral therapy. Robyn takes at least a month off work each year, participates in or assists two or more classes a year, and makes self-care a priority.

Kate sees between 14 and 20 clients every week. She teaches classes a few times a year, is interviewed for articles and podcasts, writes articles for trade magazines, and has created a Healthy Compassionate Touch program for schools with the Jesse Lewis Choose Love Movement. She also wrote and promoted her book, *From My Hands and Heart: Achieving Health and Balance with Craniosacral Therapy*. Like Robyn, Kate is sure to take at least a few weeks off every year to recharge and attend workshops, and she takes two to three weeks of vacation each year, as well.

As another example of how a successful practitioner spends her time, we present one of our mentors, Suzanne Scurlock. Suzanne is the busiest and most fulfilled person we know. She has built a tremendously successful business by following her passions.

Suzanne is one of the original CranioSacral therapy instructors, personally mentored by the late Dr. John E. Upledger. She teaches a variety of CST courses for the Upledger Institute on nearly every continent. After decades of perfecting her own methods of awakening the body's innate wisdom, Suzanne created her comprehensive Healing From the Core training curriculum in 1994, which may be found on www.healingfromthecore.com. It includes a robust selection of international workshops, webinars, speaking engagements, and audio programs. She collaborated with the late Emilie Conrad for almost two decades, integrating Emilie's Continuum Movement with her own Full Body Presence work to teach other practitioners how to accelerate and deepen the healing process. She also provides ongoing staff development training at the Esalen Institute.

Suzanne has authored hundreds of articles and thousands visit her blog at Presence Matters: Reflections on Body, Mind, and Spirit. She is the author of two books, *Full-Body Presence: Learning to Listen to Your Body's Wisdom* and *Reclaiming Your Body*. Plus, she maintains a robust private practice in Reston, Virginia. Suzanne is quite busy, but she is always innovating and creating new work. When we asked about her many contributions she told us, "Each thing was just done one step at a time, ladies. That's all I can say."

Suzanne is a real inspiration; she has helped us understand just how big we can take a solo business, but she did not start out intending to be world famous. She began simply by loving her work, seeing her clients, and then following her interests and opportunities as they arose. Suzanne has two grown kids and has built everything in her business while raising her children. The entire Healing From the Core curriculum was developed while having a steady bodywork business and making enough income to support her family's needs and her business growth. She developed her skills and her business organically, with the solid foundation of a thriving private practice.

Take some time to reflect on what you have accomplished in your life even if it is not all in your therapeutic field. Hopefully, like Suzanne, you can see that it was all done one step at a time, and that those steps built a coherent whole. Everything you have done can support your current endeavors, and the steps you design and take now will build into your larger vision.

It is common for us to think that we will do this or that when we have the time. But we have found that the time is never "right." When inspiration strikes, that is the time to act. You also need time to reflect and create. If you want your business to grow, but all your time is spent filling up your hours, then there is no time left to build new things. Allowing yourself this creative time is a mandatory energetic piece of your business. It provides you space to explore where you want your business to go and how to grow it. Engaging with the material in this book is a piece of that.

Where Is Your Business Today?

Now that you have started considering what success means to you, we would like you to take a clear-eyed look at where your business is today and what your needs are today. We are asking you to practice being with *what is*, in regard to your business.

We are simply interested in how your business is faring *right now*. There are a myriad of ways to measure this. Here are some sample questions, and please feel free to add your own. Notice that they are all simple questions that can be answered with a word or two:

- Is your business your sole source of income?
- Do you earn enough money from your business to pay all of your business expenses?
- Do you earn enough to pay your personal bills?
- Are you performing the therapy you most wish to practice?
- Are you engaged in your work?

What is it like for you to answer these questions? Any surprises?

We found that therapists who are struggling in their businesses often have trouble answering these questions and sometimes they had trouble seeing the value of them! We encourage you to write down your answers, including any facts, details, or sensations that come up as you engage with the questions.

We want you to have an accurate picture of where you are today, so that you have a truthful and solid beginning. This written record is your baseline. It will guide you toward goals that are meaningful to you (rather than someone else's idea of what your business success should look like), and it will help you to put plans in motion to meet those goals.

THE COMPONENTS OF OUR APPROACH TO BUSINESS

We built our businesses following our therapeutic paradigm to ensure our ventures are client centered. We track sensations within our bodies to help us be certain that we are making decisions that align with our values. We set measurable goals with built-in account-ability, so that we can chart our progress and celebrate our success.

A Brief Description of Our Business Paradigm

Our Business Paradigm is deeply influenced by the treatment paradigm put forth by Dr. John E. Upledger, the osteopathic physician who developed CranioSacral therapy. Dr. John's paradigm concerns the relationship between a client and a therapeutic facilitator. Put as simply as possible, in this model the goal of therapeutic facilitation is the client's self-realization.

In CST, practitioners encourage this through therapeutically intentioned touch and, at times, therapeutic dialogue. We recognize that as we engage consciously with our clients through speech and touch that we are also communicating between therapist and client below the level of our conscious awareness. We support our clients' self-realization by assisting the client's inner wisdom—the wisest part of each of us—in bringing helpful information into conscious awareness.

Successfully facilitating our clients' self-realization depends on the therapeutic facilitator's skill level and their own integration of self: the therapist's connection between their own nonconscious and conscious awareness. It also demands that we as therapists remain aware of what is happening both for our clients and ourselves in the present moment, with the ideal of maintaining that awareness without judgment. All of this goes on while we are also communicating, in touch and speech, from a place of everyday awareness.

From a business perspective, our Paradigm calls for finding clarity where many of us fear to tread. We are tasked with understanding why we engage in the work we do, so that we can communicate our understanding clearly to our clients and create a good therapeutic fit. We need to recognize and heal the stories and attitudes that we have around money and its place in the therapeutic relationship, so that we do not muddy the waters with clients around payment, thereby adding our own issues to whatever they may present. We must explore and address all the ethical issues that we imagine we may encounter, so we are not tripped up by a situation that could damage the therapeutic container we hold.

We are tasked with bringing the difficult and triggering aspects of our businesses into our conscious awareness so that we can work through them and forge integrity. This helps ensure that we are not bringing our own distortions around business into the treatment space, so we can be able to hold a steady, solid container for our clients' work. In other words, the fewer unintegrated fears and stories we have about communication, money, and ethics, the better the business side of our practices will be.

When we gain clarity, we can craft simple business processes and policies that support our therapeutic work. Subsequently, our clients energetically benefit from our clarity and are held by the structure of our business. When our business details are in alignment with our therapeutic approach, everyone can focus on the work at hand.

Our Business Paradigm is less about *what* we are doing and more about *how* we are doing it. Following it demands that we develop a high level of skill. We believe for most of us it will take a lifetime to get to a full integration of self. This highlights the importance of regularly receiving our own therapeutic work!

Throughout this book, we present examples of ways in which we take our Paradigm into business decisions. You may choose to begin engaging with this process by asking yourself, "Who am I when I'm in my integrity? What are my therapeutic values, and how does my business align with them?"

The Importance of Tracking Sensation

How do we know what is right for us? We track sensation. We both trained in Suzanne Scurlock's Healing From the Core curriculum to develop our sensation-tracking skills. We find that her approach, which was developed as a therapeutic process, is perfectly suited to help practitioners make effective business decisions.

As therapists we have learned to track progress by feeling changes in tissue movement and sensation. This is how we follow our client's inner wisdom throughout a session. We have developed skills in guiding our clients to track their own sensations during a session, so they can have a clearer sense of that wisdom.

Just like we encourage our clients to track sensation to have a more accurate sense of what they need, we use our own unique primary sensations to build a business that fits us and to continue evolving and growing it. We tap into good business decisions by tracking sensations within our own bodies. We can honor and listen to our own inner wisdom while bringing a playfulness to the process.

Robyn first noticed that body sensations were a reliable guide when she was searching for her first office. She had looked at two spaces, both of which met her needs, at least on paper. She found herself very much in her head about choosing. She was making pros and cons lists and asking her colleagues their opinions. She was aware that she felt uneasy in each office, but just chalked that up to nerves. After all, she had only been in business a few months and renting an office a few days a week felt like a big stretch.

Then she looked at one last space and noticed that her body felt different there: her palms got warm and her breath deepened. She became aware of her ribs moving with each breath, and a calm feeling settled in her belly. There was nothing notably different about this office, but it definitely *felt* different. That is the office she chose, and it was a wonderful place to build her business.

Would either of the others have been bad or just as good? We cannot say with perfect certainty, but Robyn did keep tabs on those other offices: in one the owner sold the space within a month and all the tenants had to move, and in the other, the practitioner who would have been sharing the space lost her license due to ethics complaints.

Another example of how we have used the internal tracking of sensation is when we were talking about setting up our multihands days (when we see clients together as a team). Along with all of the structural pieces involved, we also paid attention to how we felt internally. We asked ourselves, what was the sensation like in our bodies as we started to discuss what it would be like to do multihands once a month?

For Kate, it was a bubbly vibration through her body, which told her, "Oh, this is very exciting." Robyn had much the same interpretation, only her sensations were different. Just like when she saw her first office, she noticed that her palms got warm and her breath deepened. She also had a tingly, slightly uncomfortable feeling in her arms that showed her she had some fear too. That fear was not a signal to stop, but it did get her attention.

If multihands days hadn't been a good fit for us, we would have felt other, less pleasant sensations, like a constriction in the diaphragm, slight nausea, or tightness behind our eyes. We have learned how to differentiate between the uncomfortable but healthy sensations that signal we are at a growth edge and those that signal true danger or a bad fit.

It took time and attention to detail for each of us to discern what the sensations in our bodies mean to us. This is a simple practice, but it is not easy for many of us at first. If the concept of following your body's sensation to guide decisions is new to you, or is uncomfortable, we suggest starting small—with discrete and low-stakes decisions. Build up your sensation library by keeping a record of what you felt before you made a decision, how it felt to follow through with an action, and what the outcome of that decision was.

Tracking sensation has now become routine for us. We use it with big decisions and also for day-to-day mundane matters. As our businesses change, we rely on our sense of ourselves to guide our decisions. We have felt our way into knowing how many clients to see in a day, how many days to work in a week, what new endeavors to pursue, and what types of downtime and support we need.

We pair our use of this internal guidance with a simple way of setting goals and keeping ourselves accountable.

Goal Setting and Accountability

What is the result you want? This is an important question that we ask our clients on intake. We also feel that it is also crucial to ask ourselves this question when building and growing our own businesses. We use this question to encourage ourselves to dream, and then ground those dreams in simple, actionable steps that keep us out of overwhelm.

We agree with the phrase "you get what you measure for," which is one of the reasons we asked you to think about what success means to you right now. We can measure moment to moment by tracking sensation and learning what feels right for us. However, once we begin to make changes, how do we know that those changes are beginning to stick and that we are really getting the results we want?

We do this by setting measurable goals for the different aspects of our businesses and then scheduling consistent times to check in on our progress toward those goals. Just like our clients may not go from having frequent migraines to being completely symptom free after one session, it takes time, adjustment, and fine tuning as we go.

This approach keeps us from being overwhelmed and also lets us course correct on the fly, as we see the results that we are getting from our efforts. Here are three questions to consider. Each of them is vital to your success.

- What is the result/big dream?
- What are the doable and manageable steps toward that?
- How do you keep track?

We like this quote by Dr. John E. Upledger, "The shortest distance between two points is an intention." So with that in mind, let's look at a simple method of using a weekly goal card, an idea from our expert Anne Sagendorph-Moon. Anne brings 30 years of corporate and entrepreneurial coaching to her training. You can find her work on www.annesagendorphmoon.com. She believes that all of us deserve to grow our businesses and make money without hurting ourselves or others. As Anne says, "Your business at its best nourishes you, uplifts your spirit, and fills you with well-being, excitement, joy, and peace. You become an inspiration to everyone you meet. You change the world just by showing up!"

Anne's goal card practice is a gentle, clear way to declare the results we want, to stay in the present moment, and to track our progress over time. It is also something of a game, so it makes what could be really nerve-wracking into something you might just look forward to!

Take a look at our sample goal card. An index card is the perfect size for this. You will see the date at the very top center. On the left-hand side is the title, "Promise." On the right side is the title, "Go For." The middle space is for the aspects of your business that you would like to track.

front

PROMISE	Week of 4/25-5/1	GO FOR
4	# of Clients Seen	7
5	# of Clients Rebooked/Newly Booked	8
2	# of conversations about my work	4
2 days	Meditation before workday	3 days

back

My intentions for the week:
I enjoy serving my clients and am easily able to keep my time containers. My work comes up in conversations naturally, and I convey my excitement and love of this work with ease. I ask meaningful questions and tailor my answers to people's curiosity and needs.
I commit to practices that enable me to be present for myself and my clients. I will track how moving my meditation practice to before work affects my mood and my clients' results.

Sample Goal Card

When Robyn was first building her practice, she had three clients a week that she could count on. So, on her goal card, one category was "Clients Seen" and she would enter "3" as her "Promise" because she knew she could pretty much count on making that number. The "Go For" is meant to be a bit of a stretch. She would not put down 20 clients in that category if she knew she could count on three, but she might enter "5" or "6."

Here is a great place to use your sensation tracking skills to see what feels like a bit of excitement. What does excitement feel like in your body? What sensations can you identify? Can you differentiate that set of sensations from overwhelm? Each of us will have a unique way of sensing, but generally excitement has a pleasant component to it, even if it comes with sensations that are uncomfortable or challenging. Overwhelm generally will not have pleasant components, and often present with telltale signs such as numbness or the sense that you cannot breathe.

A goal card should have between three and five goals. Fewer than that and the game can get a bit boring. More than that becomes overwhelming, at least in our experience. In business building mode, you may wish to include categories such as "Clients Seen," "Number of Clients Rebooked," and "Number of People I Will Talk with About My Business." Talking to people about her business was really hard for Robyn in the beginning, so at first, she promised to talk to just one person each week. It could be a person she knew, like a friend or relative. Then her "Go For" was three people.

Once she had hit her promise, she knew she was stretching into new territory and she began to notice what that felt like. When she began reaching her "Go For" numbers, it was time to move that number to the "Promise" category and stretch a little farther. This is a process of setting intentions and meeting goals, but also one of getting more familiar (and friendly) with the unavoidable sensations of discomfort that accompany growth and expansion.

On the back of your goal card, you will write how you want to feel as you are going through your week. This could look like: "Tracking these goals is really effortless. I plan to enjoy seeing all of my clients.

I'm looking forward to that lunch I have set up with my friend Jane where we'll brainstorm about marketing." These are short lines to fit in a small space, so choose words that set the intention for how your feelings are going to be during the week.

Once you have completed your goal card for the week, take a look through it and then store it somewhere—not in front of your face, not on your mirror, and not where you are going to pass it five times a day. Put it away. Your inner wisdom already knows what you have set in motion. Then at the end of the week when you have a fresh, new goal card ready to fill out, take out your goal card from the past week and take a look at how you did. We recommend doing this at the same time each week. We suggest completing it by hand so that you get the proven benefits of writing that include increased creativity, enhanced memory, and better problem solving.

Here is the game: let's say you promised three clients and your go-for was six. How many clients did you actually see? Write that number down on that category line. Do the same for all the categories. No judgment, just a declaration of what happened. Read over your intentions on the back. How close did you come? Make a note (sometimes just a smiley face to indicate that the week really did go as intended is enough). Keep your cards, and review them all in a month or two. Over time, you will see how much closer you get to hitting your goals, and you will gain a better sense of how well you are setting goals too. Are they simple enough or do you need to break them down into more manageable steps?

One of our students took to the goal setting idea with a lot of gusto, and then reported feeling completely overwhelmed. When we asked her to share her goals, she answered with: "Mailing List," "Marketing Strategy," "New Clinic." These are simple phrases, but once we found out she had no pieces in place for any of them and was overbooked in her current clinic, we pointed out these were actually enormous projects! We recommended that she begin carving into these projects by creating discrete and measurable actions.

For instance, with the "Mailing List" category, one action could be "researching companies, choosing, and signing up." The promise could be a day (promise to do it by Saturday, go for getting it done a few days earlier). The next week's Mailing List goal could be "import list and create a template." This student reported a few weeks later that breaking down goals to their most basic steps helped to keep her calm and to keep her expectations of what she could accomplish in a week reasonable. She worked toward completing complex projects one bite at a time.

Goals are not about failing! But so many of us set goals as if we intend to let ourselves down. We make them vague or too grand, and we do not take the time to think through the steps needed to achieve big things. Well-set and deeply considered goals give us a way to break large pieces of our business growth into small, manageable, and measurable steps. Setting a promise that we know we can achieve and a go-for that is a bit of a stretch creates more of a sense of adventure, with some built-in safety. We may still feel fear or anxiety, but the excitement will crop up too.

There is a difference between a goal and a wish. Wishes are wonderful, and they are utterly out of our control. That is why wishes are granted, not earned. Wishing for clients to call is not something we can act on. Making calls ourselves, sending letters or emails to former clients, and speaking to the people we encounter in daily life a certain number of times each week are things that we have agency in doing. Measuring these things is the real point of the goal card: bringing ourselves to accountability in taking the necessary steps to build our businesses.

Kate remembers how her mentor, Wayne Dyer, used to describe this idea. He would say that in any given moment we have endless possibilities, and if we have set a goal with clear intentions, then we will be able to recognize when a choice toward that goal becomes available. We can make that choice in the moment, and so we would move toward achieving our goal. If what we are looking for has not been identified clearly, then those moments of choice can easily pass us by without our even knowing.

You may want to find a partner to share your goals with and to hold each other accountable in a supportive way. It is an added incentive to fill out your goal cards when you know you are going to have a call about it at the end of the week or the end of the month! We recommend that you have a conversation about how you would like to be supported, because many people view goal keeping as a reward/punishment activity. Remember that this is meant to engage your own inner guidance, so it will probably not be useful if you get asked a lot of questions about why you did not achieve your goals or why you set them the way you did (because that is not the point).

When Kate was working on the essay portion of her Diplomate certification in CST, she met every two weeks with her colleague, Kathy. They would report on their progress, let each other know whether they had answered the questions they each had committed to, and then set their next goals. They also set goals for the number of clients that they wanted to see in the coming week. They would share their stats with each other over a cup of coffee and make an enjoyable time of it.

Kate and Kathy supported each other through the rough patches in writing their exams, building their client bases, and when they inevitably missed the mark. They also celebrated when they hit their goals, when they had success in what they were working toward, and when something exciting happened. If you find yourself consistently unable to be accountable in this way, then it is likely that there is a deep-seated structure of limitation or limiting belief behind it. This is where some one-on-one therapy can be useful to identify and address the barrier you may have to taking productive action.

We assert that none of us are in competition with one another. We prefer to set our sights by the Latin root of the word competition, *competere*, which means "to strive in common." There are more than enough clients for all of us. We each can have a successful business and acknowledge that our colleagues' success supports our own. Everyone in the world should be receiving skilled therapeutic work, right? So we are all needed to play our parts.

Now that we are clearer about the foundational aspects of business success, we will take a look at how setting up a strong Business Container positions us for success.

Let's Get into Action...

QUESTIONS TO DEVELOP THE FOUNDATIONAL ELEMENTS OF YOUR BUSINESS SUCCESS

- How do I define a successful business for this week? In one month? In the next three months?

- When I read my definition does it make my bells and whistles go off? Is this exciting to me?

- Where do I have good clarity in my business? What areas are murky or frightening? Are there issues in my business I resist examining?

- What are the sensations in my body when something is a good fit? A healthy stretch? How do those sensations differ from those of overwhelm or danger?

- Are my goals manageable and measurable? How will I use goal cards to achieve them?

- Am I accountable to myself for my actions? Who would I choose as my accountability partner?

CHAPTER 2

CREATING YOUR BUSINESS CONTAINER

————————

Once we become clear on the structure of our business—the where, when, and how of it—we can spend less time wondering about how our business is doing and give more attention to serving our clients, recharging, and enjoying our free time. We spend much less effort managing the nuts and bolts of our business because we put systems in place that meet our needs. These systems match our unique ways of thinking and tracking details, so they are easy for us to maintain.

THE IMPORTANCE OF THE BUSINESS CONTAINER

When the details of our business are all sorted out and clearly communicated, then our clients are held by that structure. This is what we call the Business Container. Having a well-defined Business Container serves us and our clients too, because everyone's focus can be on the therapeutic process.

To be an effective solo practitioner, we have found it is as important to have a supportive Business Container as it is to have a well-defined therapeutic container. Our well-honed business skills are directly related to our clients' excellent therapeutic results because they help our clients feel safe. Clients know what to expect from us regarding business details, and they are clear on what is expected of them.

This sense of safety supports the establishment of trust, which is vital for a successful therapeutic outcome. Imagine a practitioner who has a great therapeutic skill set but repeatedly reschedules client appointments. Over a short period of time, this will erode trust because the therapist is demonstrating that they are not dependable, no matter how skillful they are in session. A supportive and consistent business structure demonstrates a therapist's commitment to their work and their clients.

Clients show us their commitment to their own work by how they respond to our Business Container. For instance, a client who repeatedly reschedules at the last minute, or who does not show up for appointments and expects not to pay, is not a good fit for our business. They are likely not a good fit therapeutically either.

We describe the categories we find to be significant (and you may think of some that we have not yet identified). We hope that by now you recognize that our emphasis is on honoring what you are comfortable with and how you want to set things up. Our ideas are meant to give you a springboard to help you look at what works for you now and to help you get clear about the kinds of structures you want to put in place in the future.

THE WHERE

We all need a space to ply our trade, and where we work affects when we can see clients and the types of people we can see.

Kate began her private practice renting a room part-time in a chiropractor's office. After the birth of her twins, she took a break from seeing clients and gave up that space. When she returned to work, she rented space from an aesthetician one day a week and then increased to two days as her twins got older. When her children went to school five days a week, she rented her own full-time office in the same complex, so that she would have more time to see clients. She noticed that each time she responded to changes in her personal life her business grew, and the connections she made within her community continued to expand.

Once Kate's book *From My Hands and Heart: Achieving Health and Balance with Craniosacral Therapy* was published, this created a new situation to respond to. She then needed time to be interviewed and teach online classes based on the book. Kate recognized that to accommodate these changes and respond to her family's evolving needs, she was best served by having a home office. One of the reasons she was comfortable doing this was that she was able to create a space where her clients had their own entrance. This gave her more flexibility in her schedule, allowed her to be interviewed between clients in an environment that was quiet and had reliable internet access, and it meant she could transition more quickly from office hours to home time.

Robyn started seeing clients in the living room of her 400 square foot apartment and in clients' homes. She quickly discovered that in the time she spent traveling from house to house and making sure her living room was spotless and professional looking, she could see enough clients to pay for renting a shared commercial space. Over the years, she has gone from sharing an office with several practitioners to participating in a holistic healing center to committing to long-term leases on her own office.

Robyn recently moved to an office at the top of a flight of stairs. It is a beautiful, quiet space that meets all her current needs, but it also means that she can no longer see clients who use wheelchairs or are on crutches after an injury. Robyn is happy that she has skilled colleagues nearby who can accommodate clients with such needs.

Every location has its positive attributes and its drawbacks, and we will never be able to please everyone. Many of us make assumptions about work spaces—a solo office will be lonely, unsafe or make us less available to our colleagues, a shared space will save us money, working in a center with other practitioners will automatically generate referrals and camaraderie, working at home will be less expensive and more convenient than working in an office.

In truth, none of these is a given. For instance, Robyn has closer relationships with colleagues now than when she was at the holistic healing center. Her clients were not often good fits for the other practitioners in that building, their clients were not good fits for her, and the mandatory staff meetings took up time that she would rather have spent seeing clients (or taking a hike!). So it is best to spend some time figuring out what works well for you and parsing out the qualities you need to do your best work.

When considering where you will work, look at all the costs and benefits you can think of. Here is a partial list to get you started:

- How much time does it take you to get to and from the space?
- What is the cost to rent?
- How much control do you have over temperature, décor, schedule, and noise levels?
- How much storage do you need for linens, forms, charts, etc.?

- What are your personal boundaries around having clients in your home or sharing an office?

You will also want to keep in mind client needs:

- Can clients find your location without confusion?
- Is the space easily maneuvered with no trip-ping hazards?
- Is it safe to park or walk from transit?
- Does the space have appropriate visual and sound privacy?
- If you work at night, is the area well lit?

If you work with clients remotely, then it is important to consider how well your space fits your and your clients' needs. Those who work by phone need a robust audio connection with minimal background noise. Those who work via video link have the added need of creating a background that is not distracting.

We hope you see from our varied experiences that there is not one ideal office, just situations and settings that fit our needs at moments in time. Taking stock of your own needs as well as your clients' will help you decide on the best location. You will likely notice that change is constant, so we encourage you to review your needs on a regular basis and respond to them accordingly.

THE WHEN

Setting Your Schedule

Most of us base our session lengths and the break between sessions on what other people do. For instance, if everyone you know offers 60- and 90-minute sessions with a half hour break in between each session, it may seem like that is just how things are done. We have found that successful practitioners find session lengths that match how they work best and that there is a wide range of possibilities.

Seasoned practitioners told us both that we would always need to see clients on weekends and in the evenings to make ends meet. That is what they did, so they told us that is just how it is done. When you are initially building your business, you may wish to work evenings and weekends, since that is when the widest range of people are available. But we want you to know it is not a rule, and it is not required.

When you start to take a look at your schedule, we recommend that you consider what you need for yourself in terms of your self-care and how you best work. Right now, Kate is limited in her working hours because she has two children in school. What works best for her these days are back-to-back, 50-55 minute sessions scheduled on the hour starting at 8:30 am.

In the past, she scheduled in a 15-minute break between clients because at that point in time pausing between sessions supported her in developing her clinical skills. It gave her time to reflect on the previous session and gather herself before seeing the next client. In recent years she noticed that during her breaks she basically just bumbled around and did not actually get a lot done. She finds she now focuses better with a tighter schedule.

For Robyn, one of the hardest lessons to learn was that she needs some variety in her week. She has always known that she does not work well in the evenings and that the best times of day for her to work are from morning until mid to late afternoon, so that is when she sees clients.

She used to force herself into a lockstep of seeing clients every hour on the hour and working straight through the day, Monday through Thursday. While that session length worked well for her, it turns out that she works better with one scheduled break in the day and one day away from the office mid-week. So she is now in the office Monday, Tuesday, Thursday, and Friday. She sees three clients in the morning, has a 30-minute break to recharge (not returning calls or emails during that time), and then sees another two or three clients in the afternoon.

We both offer 25-minute sessions for children and the occasional adult who does better with shorter sessions. If we feel a child might work longer, we schedule a full 50 minutes to see how they do. Unlike adults who usually will use their entire session time no matter what, when children are done, they know it and are not shy about letting us know! So we will prorate for the time the child works.

That is a good fit with our therapeutic paradigm because it allows us to support our young client's inner knowing of when they have had enough work. It is a good fit for us, but it may not be a good fit for you. We can imagine if our clients were mostly children, having a policy of prorating might not offer the stability we need. It could be that you have a set fee when working with babies or children and treat for the amount of time they need. This subsequently allows time for feedback and time for other guidance or education, if you have additional training that supports the baby or child you are treating.

Ask yourself not only what the best session length is for you, but if you need a break in between sessions. Or do you prefer holding back-to-back sessions? Many people start their practices with an hour and 15 minutes of session work and set appointments an hour and a half apart, but just because that is common, it does not mean that is the only way to schedule. It depends where you are in your own skill-set, and on your comfort level and the pace that works best for you.

Here is what Suzanne shared with us about scheduling: "When we begin our practices our hours may be all over the place. Once I decided I was in this for the long haul and I wanted to last, I knew I had to do things differently. I had to look at what *my* optimal time was for treating people. From a business perspective, it's really important to know when your energy is best."

Pay attention to your energy levels and how well you focus at different times of day. This will help you refine your schedule. Bear in mind that your needs will change over time! Recognizing that our needs change over time has given us peace of mind. We are now a lot more comfortable playing with our schedules and fine-tuning them as soon as we realize a change is called for.

Defining Your Session Availability

We know the session lengths and schedule that works best for us, and we are also very clear on when we are available to see clients. Each of us sets our available days and times several months ahead, and our clients can depend on our set schedules.

Robyn works Monday, Tuesday, Thursday, and Friday with her first session at 10:00 am and her last at 2:30 pm. The only Wednesdays she works are once a month with Kate for multihands appointments. Kate sees clients Monday through Wednesday starting at 8:30 am and ending at 3:00 pm. Thursday and Friday are reserved for other work projects, keeping some flexibility to add clients in on Thursdays as needed. By the time this book reaches your hands, our schedules may have shifted once again.

For a long time, Kate used the calendar on her phone to mark the days and times she was available a year in advance. When making an appointment, she would quickly and easily be able to answer the question, "Okay, what do you have available on December the 14th?" She could look at that day and say immediately, "I could see you at 1:00 or 2:00 pm."

Having our available appointments set well ahead of time gives clients a transparent framework for our schedules, and it also helps them see how much flexibility and availability we have. At this point in our practices we do not have a lot of wiggle room and our clients need to know that.

When our tight schedules do not work for a client, we will refer them to a colleague who has a more open schedule. We realize that we have to be a match both therapeutically and logistically. We also find that because we are very clear about our availability, clients who really want to work with us will move heaven and earth to make the appointments we do have available.

There is an undeniable energetic piece here. By committing to a schedule ahead of time, we are stating, "Look, I'm available here. I'm available to work." That is when our schedule fills. When Robyn was building her practice, she made sure to be in her office during her available hours, even when she did not have clients. She would study, write letters to referral sources, and reach out to potential clients. It was a way of declaring exactly when she was available. When we are energetically clear about our availability, we have found that the universe (or however you like to look at it) responds accordingly.

How Many Clients a Day? A Week?

We are mindful that not all of our endeavors are paid work, therefore we have to monitor how many appointments we need to fill to cover our bottom line. We track how many clients we can see while keeping our therapeutic standards high and our personal life and health in good shape. This is an awareness we have developed over time, and to respond to our changing needs, we check in with ourselves often.

Robyn can see a maximum of 24 clients in a week the way her schedule is currently set up. However, that is not sustainable week after week. What works for her is a schedule that ranges from 16-24 clients a week, depending on other commitments. For instance, if she is giving a talk one week, on deadline for an article, or it is multi-hands week and she is working on Wednesday, she will block out time, so she is not completely full with clients. Kate currently sees 16-20 clients a week and has created the same kind of responsiveness in her schedule.

Flexibility Is Supportive, Ambiguity Is Not

You may choose to set a rock solid on-the-hour schedule or to leave a little bit of flexibility in your schedule because you see clients for varying lengths of time. Both can work, once you are clear about the kind of schedule that is best for you. We want you to recognize the difference between flexibility and ambiguity!

This topic was one of the most active in our online class discussion board. Our students really grappled with setting limits on their schedules because they believed that always being available was how one built a business. Christa Tinker, BCST, PT, LMP commented, "I realize that I have been much too flexible, which does come across as wishy washy, and perhaps that is one of the reasons for my up and down schedule."

As our students shared their experiences with each other, it became clear that when practitioners are overly flexible it does not serve them or their clients. Their schedules do not fill and their clients are constantly shifting their appointment times. In our own businesses, we have each seen that when we offer clients too many options for appointments, then the chances of those clients calling to cancel or reschedule increases.

It can be challenging to tell a client that you do not have availability when they want to come in. When we need to say "no" we always make sure to tell people when we expect to be able to say "yes," and we provide referrals to practitioners we think will have more space in their schedules. In the past we have kept a cancelation list, so when a last-minute opening occurred, we could call people who were waiting to come in. By referring out to trusted practitioners and letting clients know when you are available even if it does not fit their needs, you are taking care of them. People remember that.

Holding clarity about when you want to work by setting your times in advance is part of holding a therapeutic container for your clients. With this comes a commitment to reschedule your clients as little as possible due to changes in your own life. We both have to carve time into our schedules for new endeavors, which includes education. We aim to do this as far in advance as possible so as not to disturb our scheduled clients.

THE WHO

Often practitioners want to jump ahead and decide who their ideal clients are. That is a useful exercise for clinicians who already have seen hundreds of clients, and we do explore this topic later in the book.

"Who do you work with?" is not about ideal clients. It is a question that is foundational to the creation of your Business Container. It is about the populations you intend to serve and the impacts their needs will have on your schedule.

For example, do you work with:

- adults, elderly folks, teenagers, children, or infants?
- people with mobility challenges?
- people who are referred through public agencies?
- people with complex medical needs?

- people who are referred from dentists, medical specialists, or psychologists?
- clients involved in litigation or insurance claims?

The types of people you see will affect your schedule, how you communicate, and how you get paid, so it is worth thinking about early on when formulating or refining your business.

When Robyn works as part of a coordinated medical team in complex cases, she needs to set aside extra time for writing more detailed notes and explaining CST concepts to the other practitioners on the team. There is added documentation involved when working with public agencies, people who are involved in legal cases, and people who are wards of the state.

When Kate had a lot of teens in her practice, some of whom rode their bikes to her office alone after school once the family was comfortable, it prompted her to encourage parents to set up online bank transfers. It will not be hard for you to imagine that these teens struggled to coordinate the check hand-off from their parents before school to handing over a check after school—there were a lot of lost checks!

When you can anticipate what is needed for the populations you serve and have that on hand, it makes the business aspects both transparent and easy.

THE HOW

How Do Clients Contact You?

Not only do we spend time with our clients when they are with us in session, we need to be ready for them at their session time and not keep them waiting too long (ideally not at all). We also have to return phone calls, emails, and texts. So we must decide how we are going to be interacting with our clients outside of session and the times at which we will be doing that.

Robyn was taught that a session starts when your client picks up the phone to schedule. When we view our business this way, we see that how we handle these early interactions is vitally important and part of the therapeutic process as well as the Business Container.

There are several channels available for clients to contact us. We need to decide how we will handle business communication, and then make our decisions clear to our clients and potential clients. The options for keeping in touch with people are growing every year, and we know that if we were not clear about how we communicate with clients our hair would be on fire trying to keep up. So we have thought about how we work best and made decisions that meet our needs while offering choice to our clients.

Any form of communication can be useful if it is one that you will use consistently. We each use text, email, and phone calls to communicate with existing clients around scheduling. We are happy to chat with clients on social media about our current projects, but we do not handle appointment business through those channels. We know of therapists who use social media to make and communicate about appointments, but we both feel adding that to our current avenues would be overwhelming.

Every once in a while, we will get a text message from someone we do not know inquiring about a first session. For the most part these days, it is difficult to get a first session with either of us, but even if our practices were not full to capacity, we would wish to have a phone conversation or email exchange so that we can get a little bit more of a sense of who is a match for us. At least for us at our current level of consciousness, we are not able to get a really good read about someone via text! We make it clear to potential clients (on our websites) that we require a conversation by phone or email before we schedule.

On Robyn's website it states that she returns communications on the days that she works: Monday, Tuesday, Thursday, and Friday. She does her very best to stick to that. If a current client has an urgent request, perhaps for a sick child, she will return a text or an email in the evening or on a weekend, but other than for emergencies, she holds to her limits.

Of course, there is the natural fear of, "Oh, people will disappear if you don't get back to them right away." Both of us get back to folks within one work day and that is timely. Some practitioners state on their outgoing voice message that they return calls within 24 business hours, or whatever their timeframe is, and that provides good clarity too.

The important piece to discover is what fits for you. Kate really prefers not to have a lot of phone calls to return. So she states in her outgoing voice message, "The best way to contact me is via email." For Kate, catch up time is in the evenings or early mornings—not good times to be calling people!

Communication by email allows Kate to respond in a timely manner. In the past she had some administrative help a few hours a week. That person would reply to new client inquiries, give referrals, and answer all other phone queries. Robyn's clients know that she returns phone calls at the end of her work day, so they can expect a call back mid to late afternoon. We both return quick texts on the fly, and channel complex exchanges (from complicated scheduling to discussions that should be in be kept in a client's record) to email.

Again, it is a matter of figuring out what is acceptable to you and how many different forms of communication you wish to track. We encourage you to take some time to consider this, so you can let your clients and potential clients know the best ways to reach you. Once you have decided, then it also becomes easier to know exactly what information you want on your business card and website (Chapter 3) and how you set up your social media accounts (Chapter 4).

How Do You Schedule?

As we said above, for years Kate used the calendar on her phone. And until recently, Robyn was very attached to her paper calendar. She prefers not to be in front of a screen and really resisted an online calendar. It did not help that she noticed that the clients who scheduled on their phones were the ones most likely to forget their appointments.

But then she discovered that a good online scheduler gave her all the control of her paper calendar and provided a lot more support. She could set her schedule just as precisely, control session lengths and times of day, and limit the time when clients who wanted half sessions could schedule, so she did not have odd holes in her day. Clients get automatic email reminders of their appointments (taking her no-shows to nearly zero). Existing clients can schedule and reschedule their appointments online, and potential clients are still informed that they need to contact her first. Kate now has an online scheduler that fits her needs perfectly and is customized to her unique needs.

A good online scheduler cuts down on the lag between clients' contacting us and their being able to schedule. Despite our fears, it actually creates better communication. Clients love the automatic email reminders, and while some prefer to schedule in person with us at their sessions, many more prefer to sit at home with their family calendars to fit their sessions in at a time that is convenient for them.

Please do not assume that the scheduler your colleagues use will be the best for you. We found that the platform that works best for us is one that is not tailored to bodyworkers, but does provide a tremendous amount of choice in how it is set up. We encourage you to take the time to "test drive" how you schedule to make sure your choice works for you.

How Do You Communicate Appointment Information?

There are a lot of details involved in making an appointment and developing relationships with clients. We need to know what brings them to us and if it is safe to see them. Clients need to know how to get to their appointment and what happens if they cannot make it at the scheduled time. They may need a receipt for their insurance or taxes, and we may need a release to share information with referring providers. Deciding ahead of time what information you need to know and what information you need to share with clients—before they show up at your door—will make your life easier and give your clients peace of mind.

Confirming an Appointment. Our scheduling software sends appointment confirmations. We both send information to new clients that reminds them of our cancellation/rescheduling/late policy, states our session rate, and provides directions to our offices. Robyn includes her intake form, whereas Kate prefers to spend a little time doing an intake that she writes as the client talks. Having these procedures organized and in place saves a significant amount of time and effort, especially when you are expanding your business and seeing a lot of new clients.

Cancellations, Rescheduling, Late Clients, and No-Show Policy. Knowing what works for you and what does not makes the inevitable cancellations and late clients easier to deal with. You will want to decide how far in advance you require notice for cancelling or rescheduling an appointment, and if there are charges associated with that. We both have a 24-hour cancellation/rescheduling policy: if that amount of notice is not given, we charge the full session fee. No-shows are also charged their full session fee.

We make exceptions for true emergencies (which are quite rare), such as sudden illness. But we do not list exceptions on our written policy. In the past, when we did, we discovered that there is wide variability in what people view as an emergency. Now, we are the judge of what is a true crisis. If you are headed to the hospital, absolutely we will not charge you for the missed appointment. If your child wakes up this morning with a fever, yes, that is an emergency.

Simply put, we are treating our business as a business. We have each had clients who do not think that they should pay when they do not show up, and Kate recently had somebody who sent a screenshot of their phone showing where the problem was and why they had not shown up for their appointment, basically saying that they did not think they should pay for the appointment. But not having a phone set up correctly is not an emergency, so Kate said, "I'm sorry, but you're still going to need to pay for that appointment."

Kate sensed this client would no longer come back to her if she held that boundary, and it was perfectly okay because this client had a history of contacting her a couple of days beforehand trying to change appointments. Because her schedule is so booked out, Kate simply does not have that level of flexibility. And even if she did, she had to ask herself if she really wanted to be spending her time trying to fit someone in who constantly rescheduled. This was actually an opportunity for Kate to just say, "I see that we're not a good fit."

Late clients receive whatever time is remaining in their session and pay the full fee. When clients are more than 10 minutes late, we call or text them. We know of some practitioners who do not and expect payment. And while it is true that clients should keep track of their appointments, we have set the time aside for them, so we feel it is the right thing to do to remind them. It also allows us to check in with them, and if they are not able to make the remainder of the appointment we remind them of our cancellation policy. Mostly, people are really grateful when we call and either race out the door to make it to the rest of their appointment or recognize that they have made a mistake and are happy to pay for the missed time.

We view appointments as a contract between us and our clients: we agree to be ready to work at the agreed upon time and they agree to pay for that time. There is a reciprocal exchange of energy. This mindset takes any punitive thought out of the equation. Having an unambiguous policy and printing it on our intake forms facilitates clear communication with our clients and also serves to take the emotion out of it for us.

Once you have a policy in place, you will want to employ it consistently to maintain the integrity of your Business Container. Following through with these boundaries may bring up some of your own unresolved personal issues. We encourage you to take note and address them when they arise. We have addressed our own issues through regular CranioSacral treatment, participating in the Healing From the Core curriculum, and talk therapy.

Peer support and accountability have also helped us address these issues in a timely manner. When practitioners do not address these types of boundary issues, they are more likely to experience resentment, burnout, and less-than-ideal treatment outcomes. Get the support you need; do not let this kind of problem create a leaky Business Container!

Forms

Intake forms. Your intake form communicates a lot about how you practice and how you view your practice. Many practitioners simply take an intake form off of the internet and do not give it a second thought. We ask you to consider exactly what information you need to care for your clients effectively and what tone you want to set for your therapeutic container. Different licensures have different requirements, so bear in mind your scope of practice and the contra-indications/cautions for the modalities you offer.

Breaking it down to the most basic elements, intake forms need to include:

- Contact information
- Adequate history to ascertain contraindications or cautions
- A place for clients to communicate their concerns, and
- Consent for treatment.

As an example, Robyn is a massage therapist who practices CranioSacral therapy. Her intake form can be very simple, just a one-page form with three sections. The first section asks for contact information, date of birth (for documentation), and an emergency contact. The next section has two yes or no questions that address the contraindications for CST and open-ended questions about her client's history and concerns. The final section reminds the client that Robyn does not diagnose or treat illness (staying within her scope of practice as a massage therapist) and states her cancellation policy. At the bottom, she has a line for the client's signature. By not asking questions about things that are outside her scope, she gives a clear message to her clients about what she offers. The answers her clients give are then springboards to further conversation, so Robyn can tailor her treatment to her client's needs and goals.

Kate uses an intake form based on her experience as a Physical Therapist evaluating patients in a traditional medical setting that she adapted for her CST practice. Her clients fill out their personal information and then she completes the rest of the form as they talk at the beginning of the session. Kate has found that many of her clients have seen multiple medical practitioners and are tired of filling out intake forms! Also, she likes to interact and build rapport with clients as they tell their stories. She often starts with, "Describe any difficulties you are having," or "What brings you in here?"

Kate's form includes these questions: Do you have/had neck pain, headaches, and/or low back pain? Are you receiving current dental work? Do you know if you clench and/or grind your teeth? What is your exercise routine? Are you on any medications? How do you sleep? What other treatments or therapies have you tried? Any surgeries, fractures, or concussions? What result do you want from this treatment? She then documents any restriction in range of motion. Kate has further adapted this form for her pediatric clients to include birth history and developmental milestones.

We share our experience to give you a range of possibilities to inspire you to create your own intake form. We also encourage you to use the resources available to you within your own school of training. For example, the Upledger Institute makes many resources available to practitioners on their website as part of the benefit of being a member of their alumni group.

Release forms. To share information with a client's other health-care providers or with a family member or other caretaker, we require a signed release from the client. This comes up when clients have communication issues, memory issues, or complex medical cases. Having a form ready saves time and makes the process smooth for our clients. Most often, we obtain releases from clients whose psychotherapists find it useful to know what has been happening in our sessions.

Receipts. Some scheduling programs provide receipts via email, though those receipts often do not have enough detail for clients to get reimbursement from insurance. Kate provides clients with superbills under her PT license that can help with medical insurance reimbursement, Health Saving Plans, and reimbursement through car insurance. Robyn has a receipt template that has placeholders for client contact information, diagnosis codes and practice codes, session dates, session lengths, fees, and all the details about her practice that insurance companies demand, such as her tax ID number, her massage certificate number, and a line stating that sessions are performed in an office setting. She emails receipts when she does her accounting at the end of the week. Other practitioners we know keep a paper receipt book and hand write receipts. Many methods will work, it is just a matter of picking one and being consistent.

Session notes. How do you chart? Do you have a paper form with drawings and check boxes? Do you use a traditional SOAP (Subjective, Objective, Assessment/Action, Plan) note or a modified DAP (Data, Assessment, Plan)? In school we are taught to chart one way, but out in the world there is a lot of latitude within our scopes of practice. Both of us use SOAP notes. Kate handwrites hers and Robyn keeps secure digital files.

Session note requirements are dependent on your licensure. It is always good to know if a client is expecting to get reimbursement for treatment so that you can make sure your paperwork meets those needs. If your licensure does not require that you keep notes, then you may want to communicate this to clients who are using insurance or who have an attorney. You do not want to find out months into treatment that they require receipts and a copy of the session notes to be mailed ASAP! Keeping your communication effective and clear helps you keep your Business Container in good shape.

How Will You Be Paid?

It is crucial to your business success that you be clear about how you take payment. Are you a cash-only business (meaning you accept any combination of cash, checks, and direct online transfers)? Do you accept credit cards? Do you accept online payments? Will you accept insurance? All of these things are part of the scaffolding on which we build our business, and it is vital that we communicate these details clearly to our clients.

It may seem like a good idea to accept all possible forms of payment, but bear in mind that every form of payment comes with a cost and must also be tracked. Checks must be deposited, and then there is the occasional (but still frustrating) bounced check. If you accept online payment systems or credit cards, you have to pay them a percentage fee, and depending on your setup there may be other costs involved. Insurance companies often demand documentation beyond just session notes, and your licensure may limit how much you can charge once you accept their payment or reimbursement structure. (And yes, we do address how much to charge in Chapter 5)

How Do You Track Client Payments?

It is no fun after a hectic week to come up short on income as you try to remember if everyone paid you or not. So how do you track payments? Some scheduling platforms have a payment-tracking function and several of our colleagues use that. Kate uses accounting software. Robyn has a simple spreadsheet with her client list in the left-hand column and columns to the right for each week of the year. When a client pays for a session, it gets entered in that week's column. If a client misses a payment and will be mailing her a check, Robyn can mark it in that week's column so she does not forget. Another quick and inexpensive way to track payments (and expenses) is to use a paper ledger.

We therapeutic practitioners generally have simple businesses, and simple tracking systems are sufficient. It is important to remember that no matter how you decide to track, consistency is key. Set aside time each week to enter in your client payments, no matter how you are paid.

What happens when a client forgets their payment? A part of your Business Container is having a system in place before that happens.

One solution is to have envelopes at the ready and write the amount the client owes on the inside flap. This makes the situation no big deal, so your client does not have to be embarrassed. It lets your client know you have already thought about this; it happens to the best of us. And it also prompts them to pay.

One of our students, Jill Ulander, BS, CMP, RCST®, saw immediate success after shoring up her Business Container:

> I … have already set many of my intentions into actions. I have updated my Client Intake Form and added a second page highlighting session fees, what to expect, cancellation policy, etc. I also defined set days in my phone calendar to see clients. As a result of doing these actions, I have two new clients scheduled this week! Kate & Robyn you weren't kidding about attracting clients energetically when you have defined boundaries.

A ROBUST BUSINESS CONTAINER HELPS US AVOID OVERWHELM

When we are just starting out in business, or have kept our practice small, we may have plenty of time to handle the details of our businesses. But once we have consistently concentrated on reaching out to prospective clients, at some point the tide begins to turn. Prospective clients start contacting us, often at a rate greater than we have ever experienced. This will bring up new sensations to track, and not all of them are pleasant!

We recognize that too much change at once is overwhelming, even when it is in the direction we want to go. That is one of the reasons we prioritize maintaining our Business Container. When it is healthy and robust, the structure holds us and our clients, helping us navigate a busier schedule with ease.

GROWING IN YOUR BUSINESS: IS THERE TIME TO CREATE SOMETHING NEW?

Let's say that you have all of this down pat. You know when you are working, how long your days are, what days you are working, what your session lengths are like, and how you are going to communicate with people. Once all of those basics are in place, then it is important to ask if you are leaving room in your schedule and in your business practices for growth, for fun, and for creativity.

Suzanne told our students:

> Once I knew what time of day was best to put hands on people, I then made it a priority to set aside creative time. An early riser, I set aside 4:30 – 6:30am for writing several days a week. We all have certain unique strengths and gifts and it is vital that we set aside time to let those gifts develop. I know that I am an extremely creative person, and I suspect that you might be too if you carve out time for that part of you to manifest.

Right now, we have built time in our schedule to sit down with each other and write this book. We recognize that it is important to our sense of well-being and self-care to have that creative edge. We enjoy being able to develop something new, something that gives us pleasure while addressing an aspect of our work that contributes to our field.

Writing also takes a considerable amount of time, and there are only so many hours in a day. So, before we began, we allotted space for the process months in advance and built in accountability with one another. This allowed us to work at a pace that was comfortable and served as a reminder that this project was worth investing in.

We both give talks and those must also be factored in to our schedules. For instance, if Robyn is speaking to a group of lactation consultants at 6:00 pm, she does not work a full day. If she does not block some time out of her client schedule, it would mean working a solid four days, then cramming in a review of her material and rushing off to the county hospital to speak. That is a recipe for burnout.

Setting Up Multihands – an example of fitting something new in the schedule without burning out! About five years ago, we introduced an exciting element into our practices—multihands days—when we see clients together and treat as a team. These are offered one Wednesday every month, alternating between our offices, which are about an hour apart.

The idea was a lark, really. We had no clue if it was going to succeed or not, but we figured it was worth offering and would be a lot of fun for us. We decided to charge our individual, regular fees so neither of us would experience a financial loss. We thought, "Hey, let's just try this out."

Multihands days have been extremely successful. Our clients consistently express gratitude for these sessions, and it is a win-win because we have found working together regularly in this way has deepened our clinical skills.

Plus, we like hanging out together for the day; it is a refreshing change from being alone with our clients. We make sure that we have time to go out for lunch so we get some social time in too. Many days we have colleagues come and mentor with us. This adds even more learning and development all around. It is a lot of fun, it is valuable to us and our clients, and it pays the bills.

There were a number of things that had to be put in place for our multihands days to be a go, and the first thing was simply sitting down together and having a chat about how long we would commit to this, whether or not it was successful. At first, we decided six months. We had no idea if any clients would schedule, but we committed ourselves to show up, just like we did when we built our individual practices.

Kate typed six months of open appointments into her phone calendar and Robyn wrote them into her paper schedule. We announced it to our current clients, so there was a stake in the ground with a solid time container for it to happen in. We created a routine and a framework for our clients to orient around and to know that this was going to be part of our regular rhythm.

We were thrilled to see that our schedule filled quickly. Then, because change is the only constant, we found that demand for multihands sessions increased, and we had to ask ourselves, "Do we give up our fun lunches to schedule in more people?" Sometimes we do, but mostly we just book out further. Lunch is an important part of our container!

Multihands days provided us with our growth edge for years, helping us refine our own palpation skills just by holding each other accountable around what we were noting and feeling under our hands. Over time we developed an approach to palpation that we presented as a class called *Noninvasive Palpation: Amplify Your Bodywork Skills*. We have taught our class at Esalen Institute in Big Sur, California, and wrote an article about it titled "Broadening Your Touch Repertoire" that was published in *Massage & Bodywork Magazine*.

It is a lot of fun seeing where these business adventures take us, as one growth edge leads to another. We always keep our focus on refining our clinical skills while maintaining a solid Business Container, so we know that we have a stable platform from which to take these leaps of faith.

A SUPPORTIVE BUSINESS CONTAINER EVOLVES AND ADAPTS

You build your Business Container by learning and defining what works for you. Then you will want to track that internally, so you know how well it is supporting your practice. As your needs change, and they always will, your tracking skills will help you figure out how to adapt your Business Container to meet them.

In the next chapter we explore how to communicate with clients and potential clients about your work.

Let's Get into Action...

QUESTIONS TO DEVELOP THE BUSINESS CONTAINER ELEMENTS OF YOUR BUSINESS SUCCESS

- Is my work space working for me?
- Setting my schedule: What time of the day do I like to work or do my best work? What are the constraints on my time (children in school, other job schedule...)?
- Defining my session availability: What is my typical session length? Will I offer multiple lengths? And if so, how will I schedule that? Do I need to take breaks between clients? Throughout the day? How many clients a day? A week?
- Type of clients: What populations do I work with? Wish to work with? What logistical needs do they have?

- Communicating with clients: How do clients contact me and schedule? Do I prefer e-mail? Phone? Facebook? Text?

- Organizing my schedule: Am I most comfortable with a paper calendar? Using my phone's calendar? An online system?

- Appointment information: How to I inform clients of their appointments? Do I offer reminders? How do I communicate appointment information? How do I inform clients of my policies regarding cancellations, rescheduling, late clients and no-shows?

- Forms: Do I have intake forms? Do I offer release forms? Receipts? Session notes?

- Taking payment: What methods do I wish to accept (and manage)? Cash? Credit cards? Insurance? Online payments?

- Tracking payment: Will I use a paper ledger? Spreadsheet? Accounting program?

- Am I setting aside adequate time to create something new?

CHAPTER 3

COMMUNICATION
FUNDAMENTALS

———————

How you communicate with clients and potential clients is the most important element of building your business. In this chapter, we will explore a basic framework for effective communication.

What we share here may seem simple or obvious, but these concepts and activities contain hidden gems that many of us tend to overlook. In our experience, all of these nuts-and-bolts basics are essential and required. You can build a very successful and full practice just by ensuring that you have these simple forms of communication in place.

By focusing on effective basics with straightforward ways to implement them, we hope to put to rest any fears or confusion that you may have about marketing. We found that by investing our time mastering these very foundational skills, everything else builds naturally, and eliminates striving or angst. There is a magnetic attraction created when our foundations are in place because potential clients are able to get an instant sense of who we are and how we can help them.

We promise that nothing beyond the basics is necessary for a successful therapeutic business. However, once you have your nuts and bolts in place, the next natural step is expanding your communication to a wider audience and we have that covered for you too! Chapter 4 discusses how you can grow from these communication fundamentals.

We define communication broadly in this chapter: using speech, writing, pictures, and websites since each has its place. We discuss different ways to describe your work: to colleagues and referral sources who have some background in your field, to clients and potential clients who have expressed interest in your work, and to the lay public—people who have no idea what you do or how they could benefit. Each group will have different information needs, and we want you to be able to communicate effectively with all of them, so you can attract people who are a good match for your practice.

ALL IS MARKETING

When we refer to the different ways that we communicate about business, we can use one umbrella term: marketing. When you read the word "marketing," what happens in your thoughts? What happens in your body? For most of us there is some activation, constriction, or a sense of moving away from the term.

What we have found in presenting marketing concepts—or as we like to call it, just communicating about what we do—to hundreds of practitioners is that many resist marketing. The thought of it, especially for practitioners who view their businesses as having a lot of heart, becomes entangled with ideas of self-promotion, grandiosity, and egotism.

We have heard from practitioners who fear that if they market their services it will mean they lack humility. Some believe that if they communicate about their work it will leave them feeling unbearably exposed and vulnerable. We have also heard from those who feel that marketing cheapens or violates the sanctity of their work. There are even some practitioners who tell us that their therapy is just too difficult for clients to understand and that it cannot be explained in words.

We wish to challenge these ideas. After all, if we are not able to communicate about what we are doing, how can our work become more widely known? And how can we help all those who could benefit from our work if they have no clearly communicated way of finding out what they need to know? The goal of marketing is not to promote ourselves, it is to convey information about our work in ways that people can grasp, so they can appreciate its value.

Again, marketing just refers to the ways we help people become aware of what we do, so we are going to ask you to embrace the term. One of the experts from our online class, Anne Sagendorph-Moon, reminds us that "marketing is a gift." A useful reframing is that we are offering an invitation to people, and in keeping with our Business Paradigm, we hold no expectation that they will accept it.

When we market, we are simply giving information about our therapy. When we do that authentically, by expressing our passion for our work, by finding out what people would like to know, and by presenting them with the information that they really want and need, then marketing truly is a gift. Whether they come in our door or not, when we are committed to giving every interested person clear information about our work, we have given a gift.

Have you ever experienced frustration when trying to find the right practitioner for yourself or a loved one? We certainly have! Sometimes practitioners do not provide much information about themselves or their work, so it is hard to know what we are getting into before scheduling an appointment. Sometimes they do not even return calls or emails. By communicating clearly with everyone who inquires about our work, we are helping people manage what can be a hard and frustrating process. Any time we can help someone find a good practitioner, even if it is not us, it is a gift.

One of our students, Anna Maria Irvine, DC, had this to say:

> I've been noticing how I disregulate myself by going into "marketing think" in a way that creates overwhelm. I can just shift my attention around that, call it "communication about what I can offer, and my excitement about the work." When I do that, my experience becomes more coherent and regulated again.

WORD OF MOUTH

Developing good "word of mouth" means providing information that allows people to understand your work and express its value to the people they know. This is *the* most important and most effective type of marketing. And this is the one place in the book where we have an imperative: you simply must do this to build your business! We know of no way around it: you *must* find ways to talk to people about your work.

Many of us hold tight to the fantasy of just hanging up a shingle (or creating a website) and then somehow having clients magically find us—no talking required. We had dozens of students who had been struggling in their businesses for years (some for them for more than a decade). The one thing that they all had in common was a reluctance to talk about their work to create word-of-mouth referrals. Yet once they began talking, every one of their businesses grew.

Creating word of mouth means talking to your friends, to your colleagues, and to people you meet as you go about your day. It is not about promoting yourself—it is about sharing your passion for your work. People love when they hear somebody sharing their enthusiasm in a way that connects with their own interests and needs.

While the particular person you are talking to in the moment might not be the next client who walks in your door, we know from all of our experiences that the more you share what you are passionate about, the more people will come through your door. There is an energy that supports you when you communicate in a way that allows people to get their questions answered and allows them to really have an experience of who you are and what you offer. When someone in their circle has a need for your services, then the people you have talked to will remember your passion and your clarity, and send them to you.

We have talked about having no agenda and staying in the present moment as part of our Business Paradigm. Therefore, when we talk about our work we are walking that talk by not being attached to whether or not someone decides to schedule with us. How do we do that? By focusing on their needs rather than our own. We keep our focus on what the person we are talking with might want to know and how we can provide that information in a useful way, rather than what we might want from them.

Develop and Maintain a Client-Centered Mindset

One good question to ask yourself is, "Which do I value more—being understood or being perceived as gifted and unique?" Over our years in the field of therapeutic bodywork we have heard phrases such as, "This work is mysterious," "It's beyond words," "I can't possibly explain what I do, you'll just have to experience it," and "I do not work like anyone else. I have developed my own special blend of techniques."

We would argue that although phrases like these may convey a truth for some practitioners, they provide only limited information for a potential client to decide whether or not they should come in for a session. Put yourself in a potential client's shoes and imagine what phrases could create a desire to come see you and motivation to book an appointment.

How we talk about the therapy we do is vital for our business growth (and, we would argue, for our clinical outcomes). Effective communication demands honesty, a willingness to be seen, fine-tuned listening skills, and a message that is received and understood. We have found the most effective approach is to keep communication focused on the person we are speaking with and answering the questions they have. Once you begin talking with someone about your work, it is likely they will wonder if you can help them or someone they care about. Asking if they have an issue or concern is a perfect opening to share more about how you would work with them.

Most of the time, folks are not that interested in who we are or the particulars of our therapy, they just want to know what we can do for them. We are not typically asked questions about ourselves or the details of our therapy until clients have been receiving treatment for some time and are getting good results!

Think ahead of time about common client issues and how your therapeutic approach addresses them. This will help you be ready to speak with potential clients. To get your creative juices flowing, you might consider how you would answer the following questions:

- What are the results your clients tell you they get from your work?
- What are the results you have achieved as a client, or the results you have seen with this work as a practitioner?
- What brought your current clients to see you?

Craft an Elevator Speech (or several)

Another big piece of your communication is your elevator speech, which is marketing talk for the stuff you can say about your work in the time it takes you to ride an elevator with someone you do not already know. We find that ours varies depending on context.

We do not have a single speech memorized because we take into account the person in front of us and the level of interest we see in their eyes. Again, we aim to stay in the present moment and meet our potential client's need for information that is meaningful to them, but we do have several phrases and approaches that we rely on to convey the value of our work.

It may be useful to have a definition of your work ready, but keep in mind that definitions work better in writing than in speech. For example, Robyn has written that: "CranioSacral therapy is educated, precise, nonintrusive touch that supports your body's natural ability to heal." If someone said, "Oh, what's CranioSacral therapy?" and she just answered with that, she has technically answered the question, but did not necessarily give the information they would find helpful. The written definition makes a good public service announcement, but the words need to be unpacked in a conversation.

Sometimes our elevator speech will sound like this, "CranioSacral therapy is a hands-on treatment where you stay clothed and comfortable. I use my hands to feel something called the craniosacral rhythm, which lets me know a lot about how your nervous system is working. The therapy is slow-paced and relaxing, because we know that when bodies can relax, they have an easier time healing."

Or, "I'm a massage therapist, and I changed my whole practice to CranioSacral therapy because I found my clients are getting more lasting results. What I love about this therapy is that each session is completely tailored to what my clients need on that day."

We keep it short, so we can then ask about them and find out how we can be of help.

Tell Your Own Story

People want to hear why you do the work you do, especially if what you have to say helps them understand how your work can help them. Learning what brought you into your work and what benefits you personally have experienced gives valuable information to your potential clients. If you could write a sentence about each one of those things (how your work helps people, what brought you to it, and the benefits you've experienced or seen from it), you will gain a lot of insight and potential material for communicating with others.

Here are some examples:

"I came to CranioSacral therapy because I was in chronic pain and it was what got me out of that pain. I was sold on it. There wasn't any question; I wanted to help people the way I was helped."

"I had tried lots of therapies for my headaches, and CranioSacral therapy was the one that really was effective."

"My son benefitted from CranioSacral therapy, so I wanted to learn more. Over time, I took all the available classes and became certified so I can help other people's children."

Simply expressing your story, in a way that people can relate to, is a solid way to build clientele. Notice again how we keep things short, so we can leave time to ask and answer questions.

Create Valuable Conversations

One thing we can count on is that people will generally tell us what they want to know, if given the chance. They might not be able to say it precisely, but in answering your simple questions and in the questions that they ask, they are giving hints about what it is they are most interested in. So more than simply reciting a speech, we prefer to ask questions and listen well, just like we do with our hands. Once we get a sense of what someone wants to know, we can give them a meaningful answer that provides information they can use.

You can always ask questions to open up a conversation. You might have noticed that most of us love to talk about ourselves and the people we know. For instance, if someone asks, "You do CranioSacral therapy, what's that?" we might say, "Have you heard of it? Do you know anyone who's had CranioSacral therapy?" "Oh, yeah," they might answer, "my aunt had it for migraines." Then we can talk about migraines. Or if we get, "Someone told me it would be good for my knee pain," we will say, "Tell me about your knee." That organically leads us into what is most important to that person. It keeps things client focused. Even if that person never comes to see us, we can treat them as if they were our client in that moment.

We encourage you to be mindful of jargon—words and phrases that have meaning to people in your profession, but that may not be clear to others. Many CranioSacral therapy practitioners use the phrase "light-touch therapy" as if it holds a lot of meaning for the general public. But really, few potential clients are going to be interested in the fact that this is a light-touch therapy. If you actually ask people, "What do you think a light-touch therapy is?" you are going to get some pretty crazy answers. (We did, and some of them involved a lightbulb!)

Also, please avoid simply listing a bunch of conditions that your work is helpful for. Folks do not tend to identify themselves with a condition, but they do identify with change and feeling better. If you can put yourself in your clients' shoes and begin to talk about the benefits you have seen from your therapy, that will take you much farther.

Sometimes people do get a little hung up on a diagnosis they are been given. We have often been asked, "Have you treated blah-de-blah-itis?" Of course, it is impossible to have encountered all the different diagnoses that are out there. This is an area where you can start to explore and ask questions to get a dialogue going that can be really helpful for someone.

It is useful, in a very respectful way, to simply acknowledge that many diagnoses are descriptions. We will see people's eyes light up when they hear, "Oh, so that's a description meaning that you have these kinds of symptoms." Then you can ask about how their symptoms are affecting them.

For the most part, medical terms tend to be quite descriptive in telling you the location and whether there is inflammation or not. You can break that down and say, "I haven't seen anyone with that particular diagnosis, but I have worked with someone who…" We have also told people, "What my work is really good at is helping and supporting people with chronic medical conditions when the medical system struggles to help them."

You may have had the experience where you have treated two people who have the same diagnosis but the treatments they needed were quite unique. That is an everyday occurrence in CranioSacral therapy. It really comes down to the question: are we treating the diagnosis or are we treating this whole person with a pattern of restriction that results in a particular set of symptoms? We prefer to think that we are treating unique individuals, no matter how similar their symptoms or diagnoses may be to someone else's.

We take care not to try to sound like medical practitioners, because we are not. We are therapists. We leave diagnosing and treating illness to physicians. The benefit of staying within our scopes is that we can honestly say that we tailor our therapy to people, not to conditions, and we can have conversations with people that reflect that.

There will be occasions when you do not have time for a full conversation or when the context is not right to delve deeply into someone's symptoms or concerns. Yet that should not stop you from engaging. You can always say, "I'm happy to talk more about this. Would you like to contact me? Or would you like me to give you a call when I'm back in my office?"

Ask the Experts: Your Current Clients

The people who best know the benefits of your work are the people who have benefitted from it! We encourage you to ask your clients what they have gained from working with you, and then to use those testimonials to help you craft your marketing, both verbal and written. It can be as simple as sending an email to your favorite clients asking them for feedback on your work together. Remember to get written permission from clients whose feedback you wish to quote. Help your clients respond by asking specific but open-ended questions, such as these from Anne Sagendorph-Moon:

- What brought you to me?
- How has the work we have done benefitted you?
- What surprised you about working with me?
- What one thing would you like people to know about me and my work?

Our current clients are usually our best source of referrals for new clients. Robyn's preferred way of finding new clients is simply letting her current favorite clients know when room opens up in her schedule. She says, "I'll have space in my calendar soon, and I'd love to work with more people like you. If you know of anyone who could benefit from my work, please let them know." Notice that she is not putting her clients on the spot, and her clients consistently report that they love knowing when they can refer friends and family her way.

THE INVESTMENTS YOU MUST MAKE

One of the most common stumbling blocks that keeps people from marketing is that they do not want to move forward until they have everything perfect, and by "everything" we mean all the fancy bells and whistles like a fully formed website with multiple pages; a social media presence across multiple platforms; a newsletter *and* a blog with videos; a catchy business name; and business cards, stationary, and brochures with a custom logo and color scheme. That is overwhelming! And unnecessary.

We can tell you with 100% certainty that the only things you need are your voice (which we discuss above), a business card, a phone number, and a one-page website. You can have what you need done and functioning in one day, and you never need to do more than this. All you need to have in place are the basic tools for people to reach you.

Of course, your business will evolve over time as you develop. When your skills and offerings change, you will want to update how you communicate. Rather than stopping you in your tracks, or making you wait until you are fully developed, we hope that this spurs you to action right now! You can always revise, and nothing is ever perfect and done forever. But for you to move forward, the basics have to be done now.

Website

Some of you may be feeling an overwhelm response at the thought of a creating a website. We are going to break this down into manageable steps so you can get it done.

An effective website only needs to be one page. It should have your name, the therapy you practice, and a way to reach you. If you have a photo of yourself to include, that is helpful too. Anything more is a bonus that you can add to your website later.

The simplest way to get a website up and running is to take advantage of the website services offered by many professional associations and training institutes. That is absolutely good enough. Most of them are free. You can set one up in less than an hour and be ready to go!

As CranioSacral therapy practitioners trained by the Upledger Institute, we are able to create a webpage with the International Alliance of Health Care Practitioners (IAHP). We have links on our IAHP webpages to our own websites. Robyn's professional association, the Association of Massage and Bodywork Professionals (ABMP) also has a webpage service, so she maintains one there too, and it is linked to her own website. We encourage you to check to see if you have a webpage resource available to you through your professional association, and if you do, make use of it (even if you already have a separate website, or plan to create one later).

For a website that is not attached to a school or association, there are a lot of professional-looking options that you can create yourself, and you do not need much technical knowledge beyond filling in blank text boxes. Website builders are good options. They have beautiful templates that look like custom designs.

Template-based websites from website builders are affordable, very easy to use, come with lots of technical help if you need it, and give you the power to update your content (text, pictures, video) whenever you want. For example, if you are changing your work hours or days you can quickly go in to your template-based site and do it yourself. Even if you do use a website designer to create your site with a website builder, it is worth knowing how to go in and edit words, schedules, and so on. When Kate moved her website to one of the template-based platforms it was a huge time and money saver for her to be able to keep her website up to date herself.

Regularly updating your website helps build your business. As we all know, anything that gets too stagnant is not healthy. Keeping movement and flow in your website will support the growth of your business. It means that you are growing as a practitioner and that you are taking time to reflect and express that. Fresh website content gets the attention of search engines too, so when people are looking for treatment in your area, they are more likely to find you (though that is no substitute for word of mouth!). There is also the empowerment we get from being able to take control of our own message and material.

Naming your website. If you decide to have your own website, you will need to register a name for it. This is called your domain name. Using your full name (for example: firstnamelastname.com) is best, if it is available. If you already have a business name registered as your domain name, we encourage you to also register your full name, and then have that domain directed to (or "point") your current website (use tech support for this). That is what Robyn has done. You will find her website whether you type in her name (robynscherr.com) or her business name (livinginthebody.net).

While Robyn was able to get robynscherr.com, Kate ran into a problem. Katemackinnon.com was already taken by a lawyer on the east coast, and when you do a search for Kate Mackinnon you get directed to Kate McKinnon, the famous actress and comedian! Her workaround was to use the domain name kmackinnon.com. If you have a common name, you may need to be a bit creative, but we still encourage you to register a clear version of your own name.

When you use your own name as your domain, it is expandable. It gives you freedom and flexibility. You can take your business in different directions. Say in five years you want to offer more or different services. If your domain name only refers to your current therapy, then that will be a mismatch for your future endeavors.

Where to claim and buy a domain name. If you are using one of the website building platforms, you can purchase your domain through them while you are setting up your website. This makes the process super easy, and then you are all set. If you just want to purchase a domain name but are unsure of how you want to set up your website, then there are plenty of domain name registry services (just do a simple search); it is not difficult to buy your domain name and then assign it to a website at a later date.

Basic Business Card

There are some folks who say, "It's such an online age, we don't need business cards." Untrue. We always need something to hand to people. People love to have some piece of us to take home with them. Having marketing material that someone can touch and hold is vital to building your business, and business cards are the simplest, most effective form of tangible marketing.

What you need on a business card is your name, your phone number, your email address (if you want to communicate via email), your website address, and the name of your therapy. That is it!

You can head on down to an office supply store and get business cards printed up for a small monetary investment. There are also several good online services that will print 500 cards for a very reasonable cost. Boom. Done!

What we have found is that by having a business card sitting in our office, when we finish treating a client they will ask, "Can I take some cards to give to my friends?" Again, it is just another way to communicate with people you do not know yet. Clients really want to help support you and they are looking for ways to promote what you do. When your client has a business card then they have something they can just hand over. Their friend then has a trusted referral, an action plan, and a way to reach you.

Logos are not a necessity! We have seen people get quite hung up about logos, so much so that they stop moving forward in their business. A well-designed logo can be a powerful expression of yourself and your approach. When it is well done, it can be a useful way to create resonance with potential clients. Yet it is *never* necessary.

Both of us have had different logos over the years (mostly because someone insisted early on that they were important to have), but what we have learned is that logos are not terribly important for getting our messages across. You also do not need a pithy phrase as a tag line or a fancy business name.

JUST DO IT (and get support when you need it)

A phrase that we use a lot is "Just Do It" (from the famous Nike ad). Sometimes we will add an expletive in the middle for emphasis.

Really, despite fears and hesitations, sometimes you simply need to take action. It is more about the energetic piece of getting something done than the perfection of the content. By getting your basic website up and printing up a basic business card, you are taking tangible steps in your business and declaring energetically to the world, "Here I am and I am ready to work." Remember that your website and business card can be done and ready to go in a day.

Of course, taking these steps means that we will be seen by more people. That alone can cause us to hesitate! If you find yourself reluctant to take action, then please reach out for support. Often, gently making yourself accountable will help. You could just say to a friend, "I'm going to commit to having this done by the end of the week," or whatever date you wish to set. Make sure you and your friend create some type of celebration (no matter how small) to mark the completion of what you said you would do.

We would like to emphasize that when we are starting to build a business, the plainest possible steps are the best ones to take. You want to set goals that are impactful and easy to achieve so you can be done with them. That does not mean your basic business card and one-page website stay that way forever (though they could!). What it does mean is you do not have to be completely formed before you put a stake in the ground.

Getting a Clearer Message As You Go Along

You will find that as you start speaking to people and creating your marketing materials, the process will prompt you to take a deeper look at just what it is that you are doing and how you might best describe it. Allow yourself the opportunity to grow as your practice grows and as you gain more skill. Then your business card, your website, and all of your marketing may well evolve.

Marketing is not about saying the right things. It is not about external conditions or outside definitions. What is important is that you create your content organically, out of your own experiences in your work. We cannot tell you how many times we have changed the content of our websites as our understanding of our work has grown and as we have come to understand ourselves more deeply. This approach has been a great way for us to track and acknowledge how we have developed over time.

Essentially what we are doing when we create material to communicate about our work is having a conversation with ourselves about what we have learned and who we have become. If you are new to your profession and have not yet developed a solid sense of yourself in your therapy, this can be a real challenge. Borrowing responsibly is a good solution. One way to borrow responsibly is to use the promotional material from your school of training or professional organization. They often have ideas and information that you can take and use on your website and business cards.

You may find words someone else has written that resonate with you. If you would like to use those words on your website or in any other materials, *always* ask for permission. Once you have the go-ahead from the author, clearly state where you got the borrowed/ quoted material, right with the quote. This is another example of responsible borrowing.

Using other people's words without permission—even paraphrasing someone else's writing or changing a few words here or there—will not build your business effectively. People will think those words are expressions of you, but they are not. This creates mismatches.

When people ask to quote our writing, we are delighted to say, "Yes," and we always give instructions on how to attribute quotes, which is easy. You can write, "I like how Connie GreatTherapist describes this work: [enter quote here]." Or, "I'm inspired by Joel

Smartypant's writing: [quote here]. Or, "As Xavier Clinician says, [quote]."

But it is always best to use your own words. In the end, it is simple: write what is meaningful for you. It is the content of your message— and the integrity in how you express yourself—that will bring clients to your door. It does not have to be perfect—just true to you.

Do Not Worry About Having a Niche

Many business coaches will tell you that in order to have a thriving business as a therapist, you will need to have a niche: a segment of the population that you specialize in and that you target in your marketing. We argue that you do not need a niche, not now and not ever!

Kate remembers getting a number of referrals when she first set up in business from her masters swim team because people were sharing their good results with each other. That did not mean her niche was swimmers. Each of those people came with different issues, were different ages, and had different levels of compatibility with her work. What she gained was great referral sources and varied clinical experience.

Like us, you may be working in a form of therapy that is not all that well known yet, so why would you want to narrow it down more than it already is? Perhaps for other types of businesses, the idea of a niche works well: you identify your target market and then you go after it. But using our model of creating a Business Container based on our Business Paradigm (Chapter 1), we really want to have people find us based on therapeutic fit.

IDENTIFYING CLIENTS WHO ARE GOOD FITS

How do you find the people who are a good fit for you? We recommend you identify the qualities that a person who is a good fit for your work might have, and how those qualities relate to your work. This takes time and exposure to many different people.

There is a lot of value in being a general practitioner, which means seeing all the types of people who come to your door. This will allow you to experience how various people work with you. Over time you will begin to get an idea about the folks who best fit your approach.

We have observed that the general groupings of people we have worked well with have varied widely over time. Robyn's first client was her dentist, and that is just because when he asked how work was going, Robyn let him know she was starting a new career as a bodyworker. He brought her in to work on his staff and her practice grew from there.

If we were to describe who works well with us, it would read something like this line on Robyn's website: "I work well with people who are interested in hearing their body's side of the story." When a client presents with that quality of engaged curiosity, we know they will be a good match. So it really does not matter what they do for a living, how old they are, where they come from, whether they have kids or do yoga, or what their first language is. We will work well together.

Here is how Anne Sagendorph-Moon advised our students, "Come up with three qualities clients need to have, that you know fit for you, and know what you promise them in return." We have found that whoever it is we speak with, by being enthusiastic in sharing our love of the work, it will either set something off and light them up or not. If they are lit up, we are likely a good therapeutic fit.

A list of three qualities could look as simple as this: "A client needs a body. A client needs to be able to pay my rate. A client needs to be able to see me when I'm available." Then decide the additional personal qualities that really feel exciting to you. As you move along in your practice, you will refine your sense of a good fit.

A helpful exercise is to think about the best clients you ever had: what were the qualities that made them so great? Then think about the worst client experiences you have ever had and list the qualities that made them a poor fit. This will give you a sense of what you want and what you wish to avoid. Then you can use your best/worst qualities list to assess fit when a potential client contacts you.

As for your promise to clients, Anne says, "The promise that you make is about who you are, no matter what they do. It's really important to know how you show up for your clients. It's very tangible. It's what people can count on." This is about *your* qualities.

For instance, in her business coaching practice, Anne tells us, "It is not uncommon to hear 'I have no money. I'm so scared.' If I was scared by that and I could not see their greatness and who they were becoming, then I wouldn't be a very good coach, and I'd get scared with them, and then we'd both be scared." So one of her promises is that she holds space for who they are becoming without getting caught up in fear, even though she recognizes that their current circumstances can be scary and that change is scary too.

As CranioSacral therapy practitioners, we promise that we do not devise a treatment plan to impose on our clients, but that we meet them with fresh eyes and hands at every session and in every moment as we respond to their bodies in real time. One of Robyn's promises is that her office is quiet, airy, and private. That is meaningful for her clients. Kate promises to be on time for each client and provide a quiet, comfortable space. If what you promise is not meaningful for someone, then they are not a good fit. It really is that simple.

GET FEEDBACK FROM A BUDDY

When we taught our online classes, we were lucky to have seasoned marketing consultant and expert (and longtime CST client) Lauren Doko work with us. Her passion for therapeutic businesses, coupled with her marketing insight, made Lauren a great resource for our class.

She recommends having an outside eye look at what you are creating for marketing material. When we are creating our own businesses we are doing it from the inside, and we may not be as consistent or as clear as we think we are being. So it is useful to find a person in your life who is not an expert in what you do, and ask them for feedback.

For instance, Lauren has coached people who tend to just focus on a single aspect of their business. She once worked with a health coach who only shared material about healthy food—that made sense, of course—but Lauren discovered that the coach is also a certified yoga instructor and is deeply influenced by her spiritual practice. She had great insights and quotes having nothing to do with food but everything to do with who she is and how she practices. Shifting her marketing to include those qualities let her inner light out and gave her audience the opportunity to see her as a whole person while highlighting all of what she offers. She is not just about food, she is so much more.

Without an outside eye keeping us accountable, we may use language that is not clear to people outside our field. Having someone who is not a therapist look at what we have created can help us make our material accessible to everyone. Lauren says, "What people connect to is your vibration and what you're delivering. It's not necessarily that you're a therapist of any kind. It's really your unique and individual persona that shines through and it's about tapping into that." She reminds us that marketing "is about building a relationship and a community."

Use the tools that we have discussed in this chapter to build those relationships and your therapeutic community. Once you have these solidly in place, we recommend you celebrate (Well done! Congratulations!), and then spend some more time seeing how the tools work for you. When you are ready to grow, we invite you to explore the concepts and marketing methods we present in Chapter 4.

Let's Get into Action...

QUESTIONS TO DEVELOP THE COMMUNICATION ELEMENTS OF YOUR BUSINESS SUCCESS

- What are my feelings about marketing?
- What assumptions and judgments do I have about promoting my work?
- How do I talk about my work?
- What would I say in an elevator speech? What questions can I see myself I asking and answering?
- What resources will help me be willing to have conversations with people about my work?
- What do I want people to know?
- Am I willing to ask my current clients for testimonials?
- What kind of website will I create: an association webpage and/or a stand-alone website? And what service will I use?
- When will I create a basic business card?

- Who am I in my work, and what do I promise my clients?
- What qualities do I value in a client?

CHAPTER FOUR

GREATER DEPTH FOR BROADER REACH

Sustainable business growth comes with time and experience. Your marketing content—meaning anything you are communicating to people, be it a talk, a power point presentation, an article, or your web copy—should all come from having practiced your therapy. This requires investment in your craft.

From our perspective, practitioners gain the label of expert as success stories get shared within their community; there is no real effort or work involved other than developing their therapeutic skills and communicating clearly and honestly. It can be tempting to put time and resources into trying to create an expert persona, but this is likely to lead to frustration and burnout.

We maintain that true expert status is earned, not created. That is why we are always honing our own clinical skills. The more clients we see, the more experience we have. The more experience we have, the more insights we gain and the more valuable things we have to say.

You have plenty to draw on right now from your own experiences. Create your marketing material from where you are today. If you are at the beginning of your career, use your excitement about your practice as your material. It is valuable. And remember that your experiences shape you over time and that your marketing will change as your business grows.

DELVING DEEPER WITH SUPPORT

Delving deeper requires thoughtful reflection and sufficient expertise in your field to have formed a well-defined and nuanced approach to your practice. While it is possible to do this work on your own, we found that it was much easier and quicker with a coach who focuses on who we are in our practices.

Both of us worked for a number of years with coaches whose primary focus was self-discovery and working through limiting beliefs. There was a high level of support and accountability built in to help us address the difficult and triggering aspects of our businesses. Below we present a small sampling of the lessons we learned from working with our coaches.

Robyn remembers meeting her coach, Anne Sagendorph-Moon, after she had extended every bit of everything she had to just rent an office two afternoons a week. She connected with Anne after seeing her flyer that said, "Just because you're in business for yourself doesn't mean you have to go it alone." That spoke to Robyn profoundly because while she knew she was in the right profession, she felt really isolated and had no clue what she was doing, business-wise.

Anne was a great fit for Robyn because of the way Anne really gets down to the heart of each of her clients. Robyn welcomed that support. There is no fill-in-the-blank template in her approach to marketing. Working with Anne helped Robyn understand and appreciate the qualities that make her unique; Anne guided her in crafting ways to express her essence to people in words and images that are easy to understand.

Communicating in this way helped Robyn clarify whether the folks she met were a match for her or not, and her practice filled within six months. You can see how Anne's coaching fits well with our Business Paradigm, because it was about deepening Robyn's own self-awareness and then expressing that, versus developing her marketing material from a template or to fit a set of external conditions.

Kate came across her coach, Amaran Tarnoff, a Marriage and Family Therapist, when she took a class on his approach called The Inquiry Process at Esalen. Those of you who've read Kate's book, *From My Hands and Heart: Achieving Health and Balance with Craniosacral Therapy*, will remember her describing his work. Her work with Amaran not only helped her with her business, but with her therapeutic dialoguing skills and her personal relationships as well.

Kate went on to work with Amaran privately and attended his classes for two years. One of the pieces that was life changing for Kate was realizing that it is vital to ask for and get support! The regular connection, discussion, and accountability in Amaran's approach was a game changer: it helped Kate create changes she wanted, and they stayed with her. Again, it speaks to not going it alone.

Recognizing What You Want Through Inquiry

Though The Inquiry Process was not geared toward business specifically, classes met weekly to focus on the results that each person wanted to realize. It is a powerful question to ask yourself, "What's the result you want?" Next, you need to figure out how you will know when you have actually attained that result. This is a process of identifying and clarifying.

Oftentimes, Kate used Amaran's class to do some work around her business and what she wanted it to look like. She had to get very specific about the results that she wanted, so she could recognize when she had achieved them. Amaran's methodology automatically builds in support and accountability, so it always includes the questions, "How am I going to support being in that?" In between weekly meetings, students would connect with another member of the group so there was lots of built-in support and opportunity to be accountable to what Kate had committed to.

When she worked with Amaran, Kate liked to build in a reward for every goal she achieved, no matter how small. We imagine that most of you, like us, want to have accountability that is more carrot than stick! It also feels good to call a friend to celebrate having met a goal. The exchange might look something like, "I called a landlord and made an appointment to look at some office space for next Tuesday." The reward might be as simple as the friend on the other end of the line saying, "Good job! Let me know how it goes."

Sometimes simply sending a text saying, "I did it!" can provide all the support and accountability you need. This is similar to the goal cards that we describe in Chapter 1, but it brings in your community. We encourage you to find a colleague you can collaborate with to help provide this kind of support that each of us needs.

All this focus on setting goals—and setting them clearly enough so you will know when you have reached them—is really about knowing yourself more deeply and being willing to be seen more clearly.

We have found The Inquiry Process so useful; it is how we begin our intakes with new clients. We ask what brings each client in, but also what a successful treatment would mean to them: what is the result they want from our work? We then follow with: how will we know you have achieved it? What will be different in your life?

Clients do not often get asked these questions, and they are not only empowering, they also clarify and help guide our work.

Knowing the Deep "Why" of What You Do

Anne Sagendorph-Moon offers a coaching process that she calls Soul Vision. One powerful question she asks in that process is, "Why is it you have to do this work you do?" She has seen that when people start to answer this question and they are unedited, their true vulnerability and passion gets revealed.

Anne says that vision connects and benefits sell. We are looking to connect with clients, rather than sell them on a service. What often happens is that practitioners think they have to write a list of benefits, when what they really need to know is deeper vision of why they do what they do and what it means to them.

A few lines from Robyn's Soul Vision session are front and center on her website: "Our bodies are our closest companions. Consciously inhabiting them is our most efficient path to greater health, ease, and joy. Through truly living in our bodies…we can create a healthier, more peaceful, and joyful world." It expresses her fundamental approach to her work: that we are not after transcendence, but presence.

Kate's Soul Vision session with Anne revealed how motherhood and her own personal healing has shaped what she brings to her business. "I believe that touch can heal many of our wounds, especially those created through traumatic and harmful touch. This then allows us to reclaim our power and presence so that we can be the agents of change for future generations."

Consider that your clients are coming for an experience that can lead to a result they find valuable. A big part of that experience comes from *who we are* in our work.

Core Expression

Core Expression is another component of Anne's work. There are conventional ideas of how a therapeutic practitioner is supposed to look, sound, and move through the world. For example, it may be tempting to think a good CranioSacral therapy practitioner (or anyone who practices a modality that is considered to be subtle) needs to be a soft, flowy kind of person. However, Dr. John E. Upledger, the founder of the Upledger Institute, was definitely not a soft, flowy kind of person, and yet he got incredible results!

Dr. John would say, "Don't try and be anybody else other than who you are." The point is not to mimic the stereotype of a person who does your kind of work. We encourage you to be exactly who you are with your work. That is how you can show up for your clients authentically and how you will find the best fits for your practice.

According to Anne, your Core Expression is about who you are at the deepest levels: how you move, how you talk, how you think, and how you express yourself when no one's watching. There are four types of Core Expression in Anne's system. They are listed below with brief descriptions of how each type naturally communicates.

Type One: hope and possibility

Type Two: comfort and peace

Type Three: determination and a results orientation

Type Four: stillness and pinpoint precision

You may find that you really resonate with words associated with one of these types, or at least with one more than the others. Most people do. Robyn is a Type One. That does not mean she does not provide comfort, is not interested in providing results, or is imprecise. It means that her primary talents and motivations are around hope and possibility, and you can see that in how she speaks and moves, and the way she describes her work.

Kate's a nearly equal blend of Type Three and Type Two. Knowing this helps Kate embrace the part of her Core Expression that is summed up by one of her favorite phrases, "just do it," while honoring the connected, flowing way that she tends to write and speak, and the comforting presence that she is known for.

Anne proposes that your Natural Marketing Style is dictated by your Core Expression. What most people think of when they hear the word "marketing" would be a natural fit for Type Threes. For Threes, it is an extension of how they already think, move, and express, so it comes across as genuine and engaging. Type Fours naturally express themselves with few words, but those words are really precise! Their spare, clear style is compelling because it is true to them.

Robyn recalls a brief period when she used a template for her website that was Type Two in look and feel: a Zen garden design with a sand labyrinth in the background. Despite the fact that her text described her work accurately, she got a lot of calls from potential clients who were not good fits. It took her a few months to realize that these folks did not come from personal referrals but had found her through her website! Once she changed her website to a design that fit her natural Type One style, the number of mismatches went down considerably.

So, if you are wondering why marketing hasn't felt good to you yet, it may be because you are doing it in a way you think you *should* rather than in your natural style. We have found the concepts of Core Expression and Natural Marketing Style support us in communicating our unique "deep why" in a way that is in perfect alignment with who we are. Doing this involves a good deal of vulnerability and a willingness to be seen, but it is worth it because we are able to present ourselves and our work accurately.

Finding a Coach

We hope you can see how much value we gained from working with our coaches. We recommend that you find a coach who learns who you are and reflects that back to you, helps you understand and appreciate your unique qualities and gifts, and works with you to craft a message that is in alignment with your deepest truths. A good coach also provides you with ways to be accountable for your progress.

There are, at last count, eleventy million business coaches out there. We cannot tell you who will be the right coach for you, but we can give you some ideas of what to look for and what to avoid. Find a coach who will talk about their services in terms of what you will be able to learn and then do as a result of working with them, and less about how much money you will make or how many followers you will gain.

We prefer to get all our business support—including coaches, designers, videographers, and administrative help—from people who have experienced the value of CranioSacral therapy. Therapeutic work is not a product and is unlike most services, so you will not be as well served by marketing approaches that are for products and services.

When you are starting out, coaches who recommend you create a "signature system" of packages, retreats, and online courses often are not a good fit. These systems have you focusing more on turning your work into a product than finding good therapeutic fits. If the idea of offering retreats and such appeals to you, then this more complicated business model may be something that you want to look at once you are established and have good financial security.

INVESTMENTS TO INCREASE YOUR REACH

We call what we describe below "investments" because they do require time and money. We recommend that you consider making these investments once you have a good deal of client experience under your belt and are very comfortable using the fundamental communication skills we present in Chapter 3.

To be worthwhile, you will want to have worked enough to feel that you have a well-developed point of view about your work, one that is based in the solid experience gained from day-in, day-out practice. You will also need to have adequate steady income to cover the expenses involved in creating this new material (including taking the time off from your paid work seeing clients).

Brochures

You may decide to create a brochure once you have been using your basic business card for a while and you have an effective eleva-tor speech (or several!), so you are comfortable with how you are communicating with potential clients face to face. The extra space on a brochure allows you to give potential clients more of a sense of your work.

Robyn's first brochure came directly from her Soul Vision work with Anne Sagendorph-Moon. In it, she presented her approach to bodywork, her promises to her clients (the things they absolutely could count on, no matter what), and the intentions she held for their work together. She did not include business details like location, hours, or costs because she knew these were likely to change over time. Instead, she focused on writing content that would align with her Core Expression and therefore connect with clients who are good fits.

Multiple Website Pages

Once you have seen enough clients to really get a sense of yourself in your work, you may wish to add more pages and content to your website. You might consider adding:

An About page: We believe the most compelling About pages keep a client focus, providing personal details that explain why you do the work you do. Very few people will care about your childhood, the classes you have taken, or your previous jobs *unless* you talk about how these experiences inform your work and benefit your clients.

A page about your modalities: This page gives you the opportunity to describe your work in greater detail. You might want to include current research that applies to your field or testimonials about your work (making sure you have permission from your clients). As we stated in Chapter 3, it is best to write in your own voice. If you do quote others, get permission and give credit.

An Events page: If you teach classes or speak in public regularly, you might want to keep a separate page for up and coming events (be sure you plan to keep this current).

We recommend having as few pages as possible and that you review your website and update your content regularly. Remember, the purpose of a website when you are building your business is to give potential clients enough information about you and your work that they have a sense of whether you are a good fit for them. Too much information can be overwhelming.

Newsletter

Our approach to newsletters fits in with our Business Paradigm because we focus on creating content that provides useful information and allows a deeper connection with our clients and potential clients. Newsletters allow us just to be human and share our challenges, discuss topics we are passionate about, and highlight our fun experiences.

We say that the purpose of a newsletter is to create community for your clients. For Kate, it has expanded to creating community around her book and providing content for people who are interested in CranioSacral therapy as well as for connecting with her clients. She also uses her newsletter to announce workshops that she is teaching or sponsoring. Because she has such varied and valuable content in her newsletters, her clients enjoy forwarding them to people in their own social circles.

Kate has a "newsletter sign up" tick box on her intake form, and her website has a place to sign up too. It is important not to send out newsletters to people who do not want them! And just like it is important to keep your website current, it is important to keep a schedule with newsletters. People come to expect them and being consistent is one way to maintain accountability with your clients. Kate is committed to sending out monthly newsletters and has done so consistently for the last five years.

When Kate took a break from her practice to have her twins, she noticed that the email she sent out every now and again, including what she was up to and when she planned to come back to work, was really well received. Many people sent replies like this, "I love the way you stayed in touch with me. I knew what you were doing and what was going on for you."

Our clients have personal connections to us and just as we care for their well-being, they are concerned about ours, too. When

Kate sends out her newsletter, she often receives calls from people requesting to book appointments. And since she sends one newsletter out monthly, she can count on steady bookings every month, even though that is not the focus of her message.

Robyn keeps in touch with her clients less frequently but still regularly. When she first started her business, she sent out postcards she made herself with quotes that were meaningful to her practice. Longtime clients report that they have kept these postcards, some for more than a decade; the postcards were clearly received as a gift. We encourage you to approach everything you send out as a gift, one that has information that educates and uplifts. It should have value for your clients and potential clients and not be a "please come see me and book an appointment today" message.

Think about the newsletters that you are currently receiving. Which ones do you actually open and enjoy reading? Usually they are the ones that offer something meaningful—you have an experience or you get to learn something. Whatever you decide to do, commit to a rhythm. It could be once every two months, it could be twice a year. Pick a schedule that is manageable, so you can commit to keeping that rhythm going. Then people can count on it and look forward to hearing from you.

Lauren Doko, our online marketing expert, maintains that the most successful newsletters are "concise, short, and sweet—something that doesn't have a lot of complicated information in there." She encourages you to "keep it short and simple, around 500-600 words." She tells us, "Right now there's so much stimulation coming into our lives from email, social media, and causes we care about, which all compete for our attention. Be very mindful of delivering something of value in a concise way. You will experience more success."

Research shows that your newsletter community contains your most loyal fans. They are the ones who are most likely to refer clients to you and they are the ones who are most likely to be talking about you and your work in their social circles. Since clients are poised to be your personal advocates, Lauren also encourages you to be in conversation with them. When you are engaged with clients, notice what topics naturally come up. Listen to what they are excited about or what inspires them, and observe what gets them thinking. Take note and use these observations to create content for your newsletter.

Email communications can be simple, and do not need to be from a service. If you are inspired to send a Thanksgiving or holiday letter, or just want a regular way to keep people up to date with what you are doing, you can send an email to your list by blind copying everyone's email address. Your clients will love that sense of connection and community. People will value hearing about classes you have taken or new information that has come your way, as long as you explain how it helps them.

Finding a platform to send out newsletters may take some trial and error to discover what works for you. Many of the website template services provide a newsletter service that may well meet your needs. Some are free to use until your list builds to a certain number of recipients. We encourage you to make sure that the service you choose is compatible with the service that hosts your website.

Kate has found using a service that provides her with a lot of support is helpful. The folks there are available by phone to troubleshoot with her and are able to help her fix any issues she is having directly on their end. Often, companies offering this type of newsletter service have free trials for short periods of time, allowing you to try it out with no initial commitment.

WRITING ARTICLES, GIVING TALKS
AND INTERVIEWS

Both of us have written articles and blogs, given talks, been inter-viewed on podcasts and radio, and taught workshops. Our policy has been to say "yes" to these opportunities when they present them-selves. We view them as invitations to be of service and to spread the word about our field.

We have had to work with our natural reluctance to be in the public eye, and we have had to make time to prepare, so what we say or write is useful. Our Business Paradigm is our guide: writing, speaking, and teaching comes from having a built a solid Business Container from our experience, and our drive to be of service.

As we gain more experience and depth of knowledge, we are able to provide even more useful information about the therapy we practice. When we engage with podcasters, social media, and publications, our names become familiar to more people. This in turn leads to our practices filling without much effort. The ease with which we gain new clients these days is a direct result of the time we have spent honing our therapeutic and communication skills.

You may enjoy social media, blogging, and writing. This can help deepen your understanding of what you have to offer as well as being informative to your audience. However, it does not neces-sarily convert to referrals when you are at the beginning stages of your skill set and business.

Of course, most of the time when we try some new venture we are at the edge of our capacity. And in our experience, the edge is where the growth happens! What we are saying here is to monitor how your business is doing as you add in another piece, whether it be social media, writing, or something else. Is your Business Container holding for you and your existing clients, or is it beginning to leak?

Whatever stage of your business you are in, you will always be served by maintaining a word-of-mouth approach. At the beginning, though, building word of mouth is required (Chapter 3). Talk to everyone you know! See lots of clients, all sorts! Learn who you are in your work. Build a solid foundation of clinical results. Gain financial stability. Opportunities to reach a larger audience will present themselves, and at that point, we hope that you will say "yes."

The Benefits of Writing

We began writing about CranioSacral therapy while earning our certifications from the Upledger Institute. Many organizations have a certification process that can be invaluable in helping you gain a clearer understanding of what you do and how you would describe it to the public.

The Upledger Institute's first level of certification, Techniques, is focused on the nuts and bolts of CranioSacral therapy: the anatomical and physiological bases for the therapy and the protocols of techniques that are taught in the foundational classes. This is material that pretty much everyone is going to agree on, and it is fairly rigid in that way. Completing the Techniques exam made it much easier for us to describe our work in precise and accurate terms.

The second level of certification, Diplomate, is focused on depth of understanding and clinical experience. We were encouraged to describe and defend our unique approaches to CranioSacral therapy and write about who we have become in our work. The Diplomate certification also requires applicants to give talks or publish articles. We did both. These certifications gave us experience in crafting a message that serves both our field and our communities.

By holding ourselves accountable to these voluntary exams (that were a lot of work!), we came away with a much more developed sense of what CST is. We learned how to communicate clearly and effectively, and we have built on those skills as we continue to develop in our clinical work.

Are there ways in which you can hold yourself accountable for communicating effectively in your field of work? View writing projects as opportunities to reach out to colleagues and deepen your network of connections. Try this: write a piece about your therapy, as short as a paragraph or an entire article. Give it to a colleague you trust and ask, "Does this make sense?" Then give it to someone who does not know your work, and ask them how they understand what you wrote. This process will help you refine your communication. As a result, you will be able to present your work in a way that everyone can relate to while providing information they will find useful.

Blogs

Blogging, in its simplest form, is writing short articles that you post on your website. It is one way to share useful information. We recommend spending time thinking of a list of topics that you would like to write about. Plan several blog ideas and set a schedule to complete them, just like you would with a newsletter.

When you regularly post new material, people are more likely to tune in to read what you have to say. Search engines are also more likely to bring up your website when people search for your modality (this is a part of the much-talked-about practice of SEO, or Search Engine Optimization, that people try to make so mysterious).

Remember to set aside time in your schedule to write material for your blog, too. Writing is seldom a quick process!

Anatomy of a Talk

We have found that speaking opportunities usually come up out of the blue: "Hey, can you come talk to this group of lactation consultants?" "Can you talk to my PTA group?" "Can you come talk to my spirituality group?"

We have committed, whenever possible, to saying "yes." Once we do, we have to figure out what we will say! Having a clear idea of how to structure an effective talk helps us stay calm. We can focus on crafting a message that resonates with the group we are addressing. This keeps our material fresh and engaging.

The anatomy of a talk is the scaffolding onto which you will put your information. It allows people to follow along with you and really take in your message.

Introduction. What you want to do right away is say what your talk is about. State what you are going to cover, so people are not left wondering why the heck they are sitting there. You can even remind them, if they have not been told ahead of time, how long your talk will be. Here is a simple introduction that we have used many times: "I'm going to be talking about CranioSacral therapy. I'll tell you a little bit about what it is, how it works, the kinds of people who benefit from it, and then I'll describe some of the work I've done with clients. There will be time for your questions, and we'll be together about 40 minutes."

You will want a short statement about who you are. Do not spend more than a minute or so on this. People will not care who you are until they have a reason to pay attention to what you are saying. We keep what we say about ourselves very brief, such as: "I'm Robyn Scherr. I've been practicing CranioSacral therapy for 18 years."

Kate will say something very similar, but then, of course, she needs to address her accent, because otherwise people will be wondering where she is from, rather than listening to her speak! So she will add, "And yes, I'm British and have been living in the States for many years." This is the place in your talk to address anything about how you sound or look that people may find distracting or fascinating. Consider it a way to prepare your audience to hear your message.

Then comes a really important piece of the introduction: giving your audience an idea about why they might care about what you have to say. It can be as simple as saying, "If you care about XYZ, you will be interested in what I'm talking about today." If you are comfortable, ask your audience if they have heard of your therapy. Asking your audience questions helps you get a better sense of who they are. People tend to pay more attention when you engage them. Their answers to your questions will allow you to customize what you present to meet their needs and interests.

The main part of your talk. Here is where you will spend most of your time: discussing the topics that you have told your audience you are going to cover. You will be telling stories and presenting information. As you complete each topic, be sure to pause and summarize what you have said before you move on to the next. Have a sentence or two prepared where you bring everybody together so they are ready for the next topic.

You may want to prepare notes ahead of time, so you can keep track of the points you want to cover. It is always fine to refer to your notes! But do try not to read from them. Practice your talk as much as possible beforehand and see if you can get it down to a few bullet points on an index card. This will help you focus on the people in front of you and remind you to interact with them.

It is important to present information in several ways because everyone hears things differently. Some people do well with plain facts while others really resonate with stories, and many of us need to hear information more than once. We know that we each need to hear information at least a few times before it sticks! Consider, too, that many people learn better when they can see information as well as hear it. Prepare something for people to take with them, like a simple paper handout, or show a video or slide presentation.

One of the hardest populations Kate has spoken to about CranioSacral therapy is junior-college students. They sat there looking utterly bored and flipping through their phones. What really engaged them was having them physically participate.

As soon as she noticed that they were not engaged, Kate asked for a demo volunteer and performed a couple of techniques to show what CST is like. Then, she gave simple instructions and had people pair off and—holy moly—actually touch each other. Because they had an experience, the audience came alive.

If you are in a situation where you have an audience that is just looking at you blankly, engage them. It will completely shift what is happening because all of a sudden it is about them. Consider creating an exercise to illustrate your points. People will begin to engage with you and with each other.

Before you end the main part of your talk, be sure to give your audience, in plain language, what you hope they take away from each topic. This gives them another opportunity to hear you summarize your points.

A call to action. People appreciate being given an idea of how to use the information that they have just learned. Here are some simple calls to action: "So if this sounded good to you, consider making an appointment with a therapist near you. Here is how to find one." "Here are some resources that you can read to learn more." "If you are interested, classes are forming next month." "You can try the exercise we did today at home with your friends and family."

Be gracious, leave time for questions, and be gracious again. Thank your audience for listening. Thank your host for allowing you to speak. Always leave time for questions. Once you have answered a few, thank your audience again. Let them know how to contact you.

If you are able to stick around to answer more questions (always a good idea), let them know where you will be ("I'll be out in the lobby for the next few minutes if you'd like to talk."). If you have written a summary of your talk (another good idea), make it available at this time (Offer it any earlier and your audience will be reading it rather than listening to you!). This is also the time to let them know that you have brochures or business cards available, so people have something tangible to take with them.

Honesty and vulnerability. Giving a good talk entails being in the moment with people (we know that if you are doing any kind of therapeutic work that you know how to do that!), relying on your depth of experience in your field, and expressing your passion for your work.

It is okay not to know everything! You can say to the audience, "I don't know the answer to that question." If you are able to do some research and find out the answer, let them know you will do that and how you will get back to them. Depending on the question, you may just turn it over to your audience, saying, "You know what? I don't know. Has anybody else here had that experience? Does anyone know about that?"

Kate has worked one-on-one with a coach and completed the WomanSpeak curriculum to support her speaking skills. She will often prepare for a talk by writing it out and then reading it word for word as she practices it. This gives her a good sense of timing and from hearing herself speak she gets clearer on how she wants to phrases her concepts and stories.

She will often record the talk on her phone and listen to it as she is driving around picking up and dropping off her kids! Then Kate will hone her talk down to bullet points, record it again and listen to it. Once she feels like she has the material down, she pretty much lets it go. Having the opening sentences figured out helps with the inevitable nervous energy she feels.

We know how much fear public speaking can create. Public speaking is a growth edge for most of us. Our Business Paradigm is a prompt for you to find support and work on any limitations that arise for you. As you do, you will see how this pays off when it comes to giving your talk and speaking about your work in general. The more you can speak from your heart and use your nervous energy to inspire you, the more effective your talk will be.

A certain amount of vulnerability is necessary when communicating, both in writing and in speech. It provides authenticity. For the most part, people want to understand what we offer just as they want to be understood themselves. They are on our side and really willing to give us a lot of leeway. We encourage you to be willing to take your good intentions, and the amount of knowledge and training you currently have, and to create something honest and useful out of it.

SOCIAL MEDIA IN A NUTSHELL

The content for our social media posts has developed organically from sharing our experience of our work. As Kate said to students in our online class, "I don't think that social media really creates that many referrals. For me it is more about supporting my current clients and spreading the word about CST. My referrals come from talking with people in my community coupled with my clients talking to their friends."

We know of many successful colleagues who are not interested in social media and have no social media presence. There are plenty of other ways to build businesses. Let's be honest here: how many people a month do we need to see to make a healthy living? We do not need to be engaging with hundreds of people (or more) across the ether.

Now, if you have a practice that includes long distance work via the phone or video connection, building a platform on social media may become an important way to connect with potential clients. For those of you engaged in distance work and those interested in social media, we have some suggestions for how to use it effectively.

Choose Where to Spend Your Time and Effort

Many of you are probably already on Facebook, LinkedIn, Twitter, Instagram, Pinterest…we could go on and on! Is this list making your body contract into a tight ball? People can dive headfirst into social media and get incredibly overwhelmed. To avoid that, decide beforehand what platforms you are going to use. Do not try to use every single one of them. It is impossible to do every piece of social media well. If you hang out at a couple of sites and really devote yourself during the time you decide to spend there, you will be a lot more effective.

Have some awareness about where your boundaries are, personal versus business. Is your personal Facebook page also going to contain your business material? It is fine to do that, and it is also fine to have separate personal and business pages. We just ask you to be conscious about your choice.

Kate was active on Facebook with an author page only for five years and then became active on her personal Facebook page as well. Most of what Kate posts on both of them is relevant to her field of work (there are the odd post about her pets and vacations!), with more local activities that she is involved in included on her personal page. Robyn started with a personal page and later added a business page, and so some longtime clients and colleagues are connected through her personal page. While she does post personal content on her personal page, she is conscious to always post as if clients and colleagues might be reading. The same is true on Kate's and Robyn's Instagram pages.

LinkedIn is a useful place to have a professional presence, since you get to connect with fellow therapists around the world. Every time you have a new LinkedIn connection, that person will show up in your feed for all of your other connections to see. We like this platform because it allows us to put a spotlight on CranioSacral therapy. It is just another way for each of us to bring more visibility to our fields.

Consistency Is Key

Like other marketing, it is important to be consistent with our posts and to engage with the platforms we use regularly, since it takes time and repeated exposure to gain traction. Consistency pays off because people become more likely to engage with what we post. That, in turn, increases our reach.

There is conflicting advice on how many times you should post and what time of day—all those picky details. We recommend just stepping back and looking within. What feels right? What do you want to communicate? Keep your focus on the community you are engaging: the people you are connecting with and who in turn connect with you.

From our experience of having in-person, sole practitioner businesses, social media is a good place to provide inspiration and spread knowledge. Over the years, Robyn has received inquiries from journalists via social media and has been able to provide them with content and quotes about CST and complementary medicine. She has met virtually with craniosacral therapists from all over the world to exchange research and presentation ideas. Social media has also provided us both with referral sources for clients who were moving out of our area.

Organic Reach Is the Most Powerful

During our online class, *Elements of a Successful CranioSacral Business*, Lauren Doko took some time to talk about Kate's author page on Facebook:

> What I find so amazing is the high number of post shares that I see on Kate's page. There's no paid boost or advertising behind those posts, yet they are getting such incredible, organic reach. Sometimes Kate's posts will be seen by 7,000 people in that organic reach. It is really unheard of. There's some special synergy and power behind CranioSacral therapy on Facebook, and there are so many advocates. What it comes down to is passionate people sharing and getting the word out in their own communities and to their own friends.

We do not recommend online ads or "boosts" to get attention. Share what you know with the people you know, from your heart. That is what makes authentic connections.

Pinterest is the platform that surprised Robyn the most. Some years ago, she wrote nine short lines on CranioSacral therapy. She put them on colorful backgrounds and posted them to Pinterest just to share with folks she knew. People are still sharing those lines, years later. Several times a week she is notified that someone she does not know has pinned one or more of her graphics. Word continues to spread around the world, and it is happening without any further effort.

Ideas and Themes for Social Media Posts

Again, authenticity connects. Share things that you are experiencing in your life and relate them to your work. For example, maybe you lost your focus and felt overwhelmed looking at your to-do list for the week. You can share that thought, "Wow, I didn't place myself first and I didn't create those healthy boundaries."

You could create posts about informative books that support your work. You could also post a picture of your office, sharing why you decorated it the way that you did and discuss the colors that you chose. What kind of case study can you share? What ailments have you been able to address successfully? What kinds of testimonials are people writing about your work?

As Lauren says:

> With testimonials it's not so much, "Hey, look what someone wrote on Yelp about me." It's about creating a story from that testimonial. Sharing may start with this sentence: *It has been such a joy to help one of my clients address chronic headaches.* Use this client experience again in a similar way to leverage the same content. A subsequent post may begin with: *This client found success in just a few sessions.* Sharing a bit more about the client's process can expand on why or how success was achieved. Of course, you need your client's permission.

> You're sharing stories to show the breadth of who you are. It's not just about what you do. When using this story-telling approach, you create connections and that generates interest.

Share what excites you about your work. A post may be something like, *Wow, I had the opportunity to work with a newborn baby today.* Share a bit about what was so special for you about the session and put it with a photo of a baby or some baby items. The photo does not have to be of the baby you worked with. There are lots of free photo websites where you can find images that connect people with your story. There are also free sites to help you create colorful graphic images, so there is no need to hire a graphic designer for most types of posts.

Making Connections Through Social Media

Lauren has a story to share about how connections made on social media can take on a life of their own.

> There's great community building going on Instagram. I have a lot of experience in the field of green beauty. There are so many green beauty and lifestyle bloggers there who have done a phenomenal job of bringing their community together. I had the opportunity to connect via Instagram with a blogger named Marisol Draghon, formerly known as The Goofy Mermaid and now as Rock Blossom, through a collaboration with Innersense Organic Beauty, where I'm now head of marketing.
>
> We started corresponding through email, and she shared with me some of the health challenges she was experiencing with fertility and polycystic ovary syndrome. I was inspired to send her Kate's book. What was so exciting is that she looked up a craniosacral therapist in her area and had a few treatments. She had a profound experience and contacted me to share what she loved about Kate's book and her CST sessions. Next, she posted on Instagram to share about her experience and expressed how powerful CranioSacral therapy was for her. With approximately 50,000 Instagram followers, a whole new audience learned about CST. This is how organic reach

unfolds, and suddenly an unexpected spotlight can shine on your work.

Using Video

For those of you on Facebook and Instagram, you have probably noticed an increase of video coming through, both the really short video vignettes and longer pieces. There are live video options too, so you can broadcast directly from your computer or smartphone and talk about an exciting development in your workday or answer questions on the fly.

Videos are not just for social media. Kate invested in recording a video explaining what CST is and showing what a session is like. She put it on her website and is honored that countless other therapists have shared it on their own sites. We also created videos together to explain multihands sessions and show what a ShareCare class (a class that teaches basic skills to laypeople) is like.

Again, these videos were created just for our own use so that we could explain our work to our communities, but we made them available so other therapists could use them too. We are happy that our material is of service to our fellow practitioners and helps spread accurate information about our field.

Getting Support

The landscape of all social media platforms is constantly changing and updating. This serves to keep us on our toes and provides us with more features to keep us engaged too. If you want to partici-pate in social media but are intimidated or do not have time, find support. Kate had support from Lauren Doko to establish her social media platform.

As we have said before, look for someone who has experience with your type of work, or someone who is willing to have a session or two to really understand it, so they can help you present yourself accurately and authentically.

Challenging ourselves to communicate to a broader audience has been a tremendous growth edge for us. In the next chapter, we take a look at money and worth, another area ripe for personal growth!

Let's Get into Action...

QUESTIONS TO DEEPEN AND BROADEN THE COMMUNICATION ELEMENTS OF YOUR BUSINESS SUCCESS

- Would I benefit from a coach? What kind of coach is a good fit for me?
- Am I ready to invest in expanded communication? What do I need to have in place before I do?
- What concepts do I wish to communicate?
- What can I commit to doing consistently? Do I wish to write? Am I willing to commit to speaking?
- What are my goals in using social media?

CHAPTER 5

MONEY AND WORTH

———————

Money is a deeply emotional subject for most of us, because it is so intimately woven in with the concept of our self-worth. It is tricky too, because we soak up our early caregivers' opinions of and behavior around money before we even have language and can find ourselves mirroring those opinions and behaviors—or rebelling against them—without much conscious thought. Our clients bring their own hidden money stories to their sessions too!

In keeping with our Business Paradigm, we aim to be aware of our own money history and engaged with the stories we tell ourselves about it. This allows us to make clear-headed choices around money and finances so we will not be surprised by bills as they come in. This also allows us to plan ahead for expenses.

This approach also produces an income that we can comfortably call a right livelihood. We can be at ease with the rate we charge for our services because it matches the value of what we provide. As Suzanne Scurlock says, "Being of service and being successful are not mutually exclusive."

We do not try to make as much money as possible, and we imagine that is not the goal for many of you, either. Quite often through our years in practice we each turned down opportunities that would have paid us more money than we were making at the time, simply because those opportunities did not align with our treatment paradigm or our values. We find that we live very well on what we bring in as a fair exchange for our services.

The reality is that some professions do bring in more money than others, but what often does not get factored in are the expenses and time commitments for those high-earning professions. At the end of the day, those high earners often net less than we do once their expenses are factored in. We are quite mindful of the costs involved in "scaling up" a business in the hopes of bringing in more income: there is always a significant trade-off in time and money invested (up front and ongoing).

There is a financial sweet spot unique to you, one that will balance your money and time needs, the investments you need to put into building and maintaining your business, and the income that you earn. We each find that sweet spot by being honest about money, being trustworthy with money, knowing what our needs are, and claiming the true worth of our work.

WHY WE CHARGE FOR OUR WORK

We support ourselves, our families, and the causes we care about with our work. Money is the chief exchange in our society; it is what we need to get the basics of life handled. We pay our bills with money, and so we charge money for the work we do. It really is that simple.

Several students came into our online class with the question, "I love my work so much, how can I charge for it?" What is often underneath this question is a set of assumptions about what being of service requires of us, and what being financially successful says about our character.

For many of us, being of service equates with being impoverished, both energetically and financially. And being financially successful means being greedy and heartless, focused only on the accumulation of wealth. Although those are common biases, they are simply not true.

There is nothing noble about not being able to pay your bills or working yourself into exhaustion. There is nothing inherently dirty about being financially successful. And it is not immoral to enjoy our work and still be well compensated.

If you want to support yourself in other ways and perform your therapeutic work as an offering, by all means, please do so. There can be tremendous value in giving your work solely as a gift. Note that if you do make your work a gift, then you are running a charity, not a business. It is good to make the distinction and to be transparent about your intentions, so you can clearly communicate that to your clients.

Think of any independent service provider: the person who does your taxes, gives you legal advice, or the mechanic who replaces your brakes. Do you expect to receive those services for free? Of course not. You expect to pay. Likely you respect their expertise and education, and with your payment you are expecting a certain standard of practice and level of service. We hope you feel the same way about yourself and what you offer.

Your Success Creates Opportunity for Others

As we discussed in Chapter 3, you can market your business while coming from the heart. If you are honoring your gifts and standing in your truth, you will be willing to share what you know to help people. Kate remembers hearing an interview with Nick Ortner, the tapping expert. He said that if anyone who does therapeutic work gets to the success level of the average pharmaceutical executive, he would cheer that person on because it would show that we collectively had the capacity to make a really big change in the economy and the health of the world.

Your business success can allow you the freedom to create a platform that educates the public about your therapeutic work. When you have enough business and charge enough for your services, you are more likely to have the time and energy available to devote yourself to furthering your field.

We now find ourselves in the fortunate position of not being able to see everyone who seeks us out for CranioSacral therapy. This allows us to support our colleagues in building their own businesses through our direct referrals and through information we provide to the public. It is our hope and dream for this book that our investment in writing it will help more practitioners build their businesses. Then more people will be able to receive skilled therapeutic work.

We would not be able to do any of this if we did not charge a fair rate for our work. We encourage you to take a look at your assumptions about work, money, and what it means to you to charge for your services.

A Fair Exchange

We base our rate on our financial needs and our level of experience in our field. We have each invested significant amounts of money and time into our manual therapy education, both in classwork and in mentoring. We continue to develop our skills, and our income needs to provide for that as well.

In deciding what to charge, we consider the investments we have made to develop our expertise. And since we work in therapeutic relationship with our clients, we ask what investment we want our clients to bring to the table.

Clients Value What They Pay For

To put it simply, if you do not have a fair exchange, people will not value what you have to offer. For some people, thinking of money as an exchange of energy takes the stigma out of charging. And certainly, therapeutic work involves an exchange of energy, and one could look at money as the tangible sign of giving and receiving that creates a balance.

Robyn had an early experience that illustrates how putting a monetary value to a service creates value for clients:

I was a medical assistant at a health clinic, and when I first arrived everything was free for teenagers. Their visits were free and their medication was free; there was never a charge for anything. Compliance rates were really low. Our clients didn't take their medication. They didn't show up for follow-up appointments. They didn't change the behaviors that caused them to need our services.

About a year after I started we instituted a charge for every service that was just about equal—I'm dating myself here—to the price of a new CD. That was about $15 at the time. Lo and behold, teens showed up for their appointments. They took their medications. They brought their partners in and got educated. The health of the teenage population in our area really improved.

You see, we asked something of our patients, and they stepped right into that responsibility and took better care of themselves because they were required to invest in the process. You would think that our numbers would have gone down for patient visits once we started charging, but that wasn't how it went. Actually, our patients started to refer their friends. They started to respect what we did a lot more.

This demonstrates that effective therapeutic work is a partnership. In following our Business Paradigm, we want to discourage having a "fix-it mentality." By valuing our work enough to charge fairly for it, we prompt our clients to value it too. We then inspire them to collaborate with us toward their own therapeutic goals. We create the opportunity for our clients to show up fully so that they can get the most out of what we offer.

A Fair Exchange Has Benefits That Ripple Outward

One of our online class participants, Kelly Marie O'Brien Pahman, shared a compelling story:

> Charging a fair rate empowers your client and your community. The ability to work for free is an advantage that is only available to those with a certain amount of economic wealth. I had a doula client on Medicaid (government health coverage for people with low income) who paid me less than my regular rate but paid me none the less (if she can pay me anyone can pay me).
>
> She rocked her birth. She did not know anyone else who had had a natural birth, but this mother was a trailblazer. At the follow-up with her doctor, she was asked when she was going to be a doula! This client is now inspired to work with her community in a way few could.
>
> If I were to offer the same service to her community for free, it would rob her of her ability to utilize her creative wealth and create a sustainable income for her family. I

would be robbing her community of better birth opportunities and improved outcomes and additionally rob my profession of diverse voices and collaboration that would improve the field as a whole. I charge a fair rate because I want there to continue to be providers in the field of work I love, and nourish my community.

Kelly Marie highlights a really important point to consider when we think not charging demonstrates that we have a big heart: we may actually be doing our clients and communities a disservice. Let's empower our good intentions with sound economics.

The Pros and Cons of Trading with Other Practitioners

It is very common in our field for practitioners to trade work with one another. This type of exchange can be very valuable! But, like everything about business, it is good to do your trades consciously, so that it is a fit for your unique business as it is right now.

We recommend that you take a look at how many trades you are doing, and if that number works out with your financial bottom line. Ask yourself if each trade is an equivalent value for each practitioner's work.

When Kate first examined this aspect of her business, she noticed that there was a discrepancy between her rate and experience and the rate and experience of the bodyworker she regularly traded with. They talked about it and figured that out a fair exchange would be for Kate to receive a 90-minute massage for each 60-minute CST session that she performed.

They looked objectively at the value of their work and honored that assessment. Since then, the bodyworker has had additional training and raised her rates, so they updated their agreement to an even exchange of 60 minutes each. It is good to keep these conversations fresh so we are respecting each other's worth and can prevent resentment from building up.

Because trading is so ubiquitous in our field, we both did a lot of trades when we were first starting our businesses. One valuable lesson that we learned is that not every practitioner is a good fit for us, and when the fit is not right, trading does not feel good! So we only receive treatment from practitioners who we feel are likely to be good therapeutic matches, and we always pay for our first treatment. This policy keeps us from getting into situations where we might feel pressured to continue something that just is not working for us, and that might then require challenging conversations to resolve.

It may sound counterintuitive, but we always need to ask ourselves if we can afford to trade. Trading sessions takes time away from seeing paying clients. Paradoxically, at the beginning of your practice it seems most helpful to trade, because you likely do not have a lot of cash, and trading allows you to get to know more people and experience different modalities. But you also need to build your business and your overhead expenses must be paid.

We suggest you ask yourself, "What do I need to earn during the time I'm in my workspace? I have to use this time to earn a certain amount of money before I start to trade." There are times we have to answer, "You know what? I cannot afford to trade right now because I have overhead expenses I need to cover, so I need to be working with paying clients to meet my bills." Earlier in the book we talked about the importance of being available during the time slots we have set aside to see clients. Here is a situation where you can decide if trading negatively impacts your ability to see clients or to actively work on your word-of-mouth referrals.

We have heard practitioners say that they should not have to pay for sessions since they can just trade with their colleagues. That is certainly one way to look at things. Another perspective is: if we do not value the work enough to pay for sessions ourselves, how in the world can we expect people to pay us? By paying for our own treatments we demonstrate that the work we do has value.

WHAT TO CHARGE

A Business or a Hobby?

We would like you to be completely honest with yourself about the state of your business. One way to do that is to ask yourself if you currently have a business or a hobby.

Here are some of the ways you can discover this:

- Are you paying for all your business expenses with the money you are bringing in through your therapeutic work?
- Do you bring in enough to pay for your office rent (or a portion of your home costs if you work at home)?
- Do you bring in enough to cover the laundry, if you do bodywork?
- Do you bring in enough to cover your education, including travel and books?

If you are paying for these expenses out of your personal funds, at this point you do not have a business—you have a hobby. This is not inherently a bad thing, but if you want to have a business, you will need to charge enough (and see enough clients), so that you can at least pay for all of the expenses coming in. That is the minimum. Ideally, your business will support your life: you will bring in more than enough income to cover both your business and personal expenses, so you will have money to invest in your future.

Again, we are not telling you that you have to have a business. It is perfectly okay to have a hobby, and we know many colleagues who practice this way. They have their full-time jobs and they see a few people in the evenings. They still charge a rate that they feel matches the worth of what they offer and reflects the investment that they wish their clients to make in the work, but they do not worry about needing the money they make doing their therapeutic work to cover all their expenses.

Several of our students discovered that what they thought was a business was actually a hobby. Simply having that clarity helped them get out of confusion and into productive action. Knowing where they stood financially was a catalyst to reevaluate their rates and reach out to new clients.

Define Your Needs and Wants

Having a clear idea of your current business and personal expenses is one important component of setting your rates. You will also want to consider how much you are able to work and the amount of time off you require to do good work. Vacations, family obligations, funds set aside for unforeseen events, and retirement savings factor in as well. We encourage you to spend some time creating a list of your current expenses, expenses that you know will be coming up in the next few years, and future expenses that will need to be funded over time.

Do Not Worry Too Much About What Others Charge

This is how most folks set their rates: they look at what others in their field charge and then match that rate (or decide others have more experience and so should charge more, and then set their own rate lower!). While there is some value in seeing how others price their services, we believe this is the least important measure to use when deciding what to charge. We have found that if you are comfortable with how you value your work and are clear in communicating the benefits of that work, clients who are a good fit for you will fill your business and be happy to pay for the value you provide.

A Simple Formula for Setting Your Rate

Kate has a very simple formula for the minimum rate she needs to charge:

> I sit down and do some basic arithmetic. I track an average of how many people I see each month. I then total up my outgoings, including things that can easily be forgotten like education, taxes, self-care, and office improvements. I average out my total estimated expenses for each month, both for my business and my personal life, and divide it by the average number of sessions that I do in a month. This starts to give me a baseline of how much to charge.

One of the benefits of Kate's system is that she takes emotion out of the process from the start. She has solid numbers to guide her. She is keenly aware of the variables that affect her income so she can adjust them to play with different scenarios before she sets her rates. She might decide to see more clients per month or take one less class each year. The information is clear, so her choices are too. Then, once she has settled on a rate that fits her data, she can track sensation in her body to hone her decision.

A word about rates for different session lengths. We encourage you to consider that every session, no matter how long or short, has set costs to you. For instance, if you do bodywork, then you will have sheets to wash. There is the time involved in communicating with your client to set up the appointment and time spent in writing your session notes.

Because we take those costs into account, our half sessions are charged at slightly more than half our full session rate. When we schedule longer sessions, we do not discount. A session and a half is charged at our full rate plus one-half that rate.

Bartering

There are times when clients have brought us eggs as partial payment, have cooked us wonderful meals as payment, or even made us clothing. We have bartered for services and for tangible goods. A fair barter exchange can be satisfying to set up and also work therapeutically because as we discuss bartering we are having a conversation about value.

However, we need to be mindful of what is valuable to us so that we do not barter for goods or services we do not want or need. Robyn recalls an experience that helped her understand the pitfalls of bartering.

> Way back, when I was studying herbal medicine, I was making tinctures and salves for sale. I went to a fair and a woman came up to me and said, "I'll take three of these and I'll trade you this," which was something that I had no interest in and no use for. Before I could say, "Boo," she was off with my product that I valued much more highly than I valued what she gave me. It was another one of those, "Ding, ding, ding. Pay attention to this" moments. While I didn't run after her and try to take my stuff back, I really wanted to. It's that feeling of resentment, of inequality, of a "not match" that we can try to bypass in our efforts to be nice.

Sliding Scales

Some therapists will automatically say that they work on a sliding scale because it takes some of the thinking out of deciding how much to charge. If that sounds appealing to you, we would like you to reconsider! Deciding what you think your clients can or cannot afford is a guessing game, and it takes the value of your work out of the equation completely.

We encourage you to decide what works for you, and then, should a client express an inability to pay that rate, explore on a case-by-case basis what an equitable exchange would be. To have clarity around this subject, it is good to have your line in the sand drawn out before discussing rates with clients.

Know how low you are willing to go and make sure it is not an amount that will leave you struggling to pay your own bills. We know therapists, ourselves included, who choose to keep their volunteer work completely separate from their businesses, and so they rarely reduce their rates or do not reduce their rates at all. This is a completely reasonable business policy. At the end of the day, it is important for the therapeutic relationship that you feel good about how much you are being paid. Really step into the amount that you have decided to charge and if you choose to have some flexibility, keep a close eye on how much you are accommodating.

Bear in mind that it is not uncommon to have clients who will tell you how impoverished they are yet pay the full amount. Everyone, including our clients, has money stories running beneath their conscious awareness. Again, it is not helpful to decide how much someone else can pay. It is quite possible that a client is just expressing their worry or story about money, or is working through valuing the work, and it does not mean they are asking for a discount or that they cannot pay you.

Kate has never said that she has a sliding scale in any of her information about her practice. That has served her because of her tendency to be overly accommodating. She knows that had she used a sliding scale she would be all over the place. It would also involve a lot of time talking and figuring out payment, when we want to keep the payment process as simple as possible.

We may fall prey to projecting a poverty consciousness onto our clients. We may inadvertently be encouraging our clients to devalue what we offer. This all can lead to less-than-ideal therapeutic outcomes. We do not want our rate to dominate the conversation or be a large aspect affecting clients' coming into our office. We recommend you make it very simple, clear, clean, and done.

When a Reduced Rate Makes Sense

Suzanne shared with us that she does accommodate clients with financial needs that prevent them from paying her full rate, but not on the first visit.

> If someone calls me out of the blue, I don't know them. If they are not coming with a referral from someone else and their first question is, "Do you have a sliding scale?" my answer is, "I do work at a reduced rate when it is needed. However, I only do this for people I am already treating because something has happened in their world that's made it financially too burdensome to pay full fare for a session. Everyone comes in and pays full fare for the first session. We then can have a conversation about your financial need and your circumstances."
>
> In some cases, I may be able to refer them to one of the people I've mentored in my area or to a colleague who charges less than I do. Then they can get the treatment

they need on a regular basis, and my colleague can be paid what they fully deserve. There are clients for whom I offer a reduced fee and I have for years. I don't have a problem with that, but they really do have financial need.

Once we have worked with a client and know that we are a good fit, we can discuss what a fair exchange would be. We both have adjusted our rates when clients have a change in circumstances. We prefer to continue our work, and if we are able to offer a lowered rate, we do. Oftentimes people who've had a dip in their income will need to lower their rates temporarily, and then they come right back up. We have found that these clients pay back the difference without our asking because they value the work so much.

We know that there are clients who cannot afford our full rate. Hopefully, like us, you will be willing to work with them. But we encourage you not to assume what their needs are before discussing it with them. One of our colleagues states on her website, "I have a limited number of reduced-fee spots available. Should you feel you need one of these spots, please talk to me." It is clear that she has worked out just how many people she can see below her regular rate to keep her income where she needs it to be, and she makes it known that she expects to have a conversation before reducing her rate.

Coupons and Discount Deals

We have never participated in an online coupon deal. It does not fit well into our Business Paradigm of being present for people as they are when they need a resource and providing it for a fair exchange. Coupon deals expire, which could prompt people to schedule when they otherwise would not. This fills a session slot that could be used by someone in true need. Tracking who has discounts and who does not also adds complexity to our business and is a distraction from our therapeutic work.

It can be challenging to see folks who can easily pay your full rate use a coupon, and then see a client of lesser means who commits to paying your full rate make adjustments to their own budget to do that. Practitioners who use discount sites or coupons tend to have clients who want to keep using that service. In essence these practitioners have two rates, one of them always steeply discounted.

Here is a good question to ponder, thanks to Anne Sagendorph-Moon: "Do you want to be a deal or do you want to be of value?"

When We Do Not Charge At All

Many helping professions offer *pro bono* (no charge) work for specific populations or causes, and we do the same. It is one of the ways we support our community. We mindfully set parameters for our *pro bono* work so that we are clear about when we offer no-cost sessions and to whom. We also only offer our work at no charge when our financial and time needs are met.

Giving Back to Our Communities Should Not Impoverish Us

We each perform unpaid work to support the fields and causes we care about. Kate is active in promoting the Jesse Lewis Choose Love Movement social emotional learning program, and she developed the touch portion of that curriculum. Robyn is on the integrative medicine staff committee at a local hospital. These endeavors require a considerable amount of time and energy! When setting our rates, we must consider the time we spend performing unpaid work, so we can give of ourselves without worrying about our expenses.

When to Raise Rates and By How Much?

Most of us at some point or another have had a hard time raising rates, and that is when all our money stories come flooding in! One way to reframe, "I am raising my rates" is to tell yourself, "I am giving myself a pay raise." After all, if we were employed in a job we would expect to undergo regular reviews and be rewarded for good performance with a pay raise, right?

It is reasonable to give yourself a raise at regular intervals. Some practitioners raise their rates every six months, some every year or two. You may decide to raise your rates when your circumstances change, for instance, if you are not able to work as much or when there is not enough room in your business for new clients. You may also decide to raise your rates when you have expanded your offerings or deepened your skills.

Having a mentor or colleague to talk to can be helpful when considering an increase in your rates. It can be useful to get a reality check and validation of your skill set. We are amused by what happens when we have gone too long without raising our rates: longtime clients will start asking us how much we charge or will spontaneously start paying us more by mistake. We have learned to pay attention to these signs and to take them as a signal that we need to re-examine our fee schedule.

Kate's simple formula for setting her rates also helps her decide how much to increase her rates:

> Just recently, I recognized I wanted to reduce the number of sessions I was doing per month because of our family situation and my own need for self-care. With that in mind, I used my formula and tracked my body's sensation to decide how much I needed to raise my rates.

How to Raise Your Rates

We view raising our rates as an opportunity to communicate with our clients about the value of the work we are doing together, so a couple of months before our new rate goes into effect we send out an email to our current clients. In it we express appreciation for their trust in us, and we mention our excitement at the results they are creating in our work together. We then tell them how much our rate will be increasing and when. Once the email has been sent, we make sure that we keep our lines of communication open by asking our clients in person if they have received it.

Even when clients value our work, an increase in our rates can bring up their own money issues. To acknowledge this, Robyn has a line she uses with her existing clients when she raises her rates. "If my new rate poses a hardship for you, please discuss it with me." Our expert Suzanne Scurlock uses a similar approach. "If this new rate causes you financial hardship, I am fully willing to have a conversation with you about it because I value our therapeutic relationship and I want it to continue." She hasn't lost anyone for a rate increase in a decade.

Kate keeps a laminated note on the table next to where her clients sit, stating her current rate and the correct spelling of her name. Clients like this because all payment information is right in front of them. Often people are a little spacey after their session or feel embarrassed asking yet again how to spell "Mackinnon" and they like to have a cheat sheet close by! It works well after you have raised your rates as a handy reminder.

It Is Not About the Economy

We have seen practitioners decide to set their rates low because of news reports that the economy is struggling. They will say, "Oh, well, the economy in my area has just been terrible, so I can't charge to match my value." This hasn't been our experience. The economy in our area has varied wildly in the decades that we have been practicing. Our businesses have never dipped when the economy slowed, so we have not adjusted our rates to match what others say the economy is doing. We have both had the experience of increasing our rates in an economic down turn because our businesses were signaling for an increased rate, and we have seen an uptick in clients each time. We suggest that you pay attention to what is going on in your own business and not the economy as a whole.

ESTABLISHING VALUE, ENCOURAGING DISCUSSIONS OF WORTH

Our clients are often very appreciative of our work with them and sing our praises. That is very gratifying! But it is also quite common to forget how far we have come, and clients can lose sight of the benefits of our work. A healthy way to take care of both our therapeutic container and Business Container is to discuss how clients' treatments are progressing, ask how they are benefitting from our work together, and tell them the changes we observe in how they present and what they report. Our transparency and willingness to engage serves our clients and establishes our worth.

Check-ins

With new clients, we recognize the importance of addressing expectations: we make sure to communicate that while we will know with some certainty whether we are a good fit within one session, it can take a few sessions to really see the trajectory of our work. If after three sessions either of us feels we are not moving in the right direction, then we will gladly refer out. This way, folks are not expecting utter transformation after one session (though it does happen, and we welcome it when it does!), and they are reminded that this is a process, just like every other healing activity and modality.

Over time we can continue this process by checking in periodically with a brief conversation about how our work is going for them. It is yet another gift of holding a good container. Are we getting their goals met? What is their experience of our work together? Maybe they have not even thought of how well they are doing. It is human nature to only see what is not quite right, and reflecting on where people were when they started and where they are now is good clinical and business practice.

Most of the time your clients will walk away from the conversation inspired and encouraged. But, of course, you may find that someone is not making the progress they would like. While that can be difficult, it is much better to know! Then you can refine what you are doing in session, refer out, or end the relationship. Any way it goes, you are still taking good care of your client, and clients appreciate the check-in and that you value their getting what they need. We also find that these conversations increase our own clinical skill, because we get feedback that we may not otherwise receive.

How We Take Payment

One way we uphold the worth of our work is by making payment and scheduling clear for our clients. Our very practical clients who really take good care of themselves will come in, put down their check (all filled out) right at the beginning and say, "Can we make our next appointment now?" These people are shining examples of how to take good care of oneself, because they are respecting their own time and value the time container for their work.

We can help model that for our clients. It is a service to ask clients as they walk in the door, "Do want to reschedule now before we get to work?" You may want to guide your clients who are really spacey at the end of a session by saying, "Next time you may want to pay me at the beginning, if that feels good to you. That way you don't have to start doing those practical left-brain things at the end." Payment is just a part of the work, and the more matter-of-fact we can be about it, the less stressful it is for our clients.

What do you do when somebody is about to walk out the door and they have not paid you? It can be an awkward moment. Simply asking, "How would you like to pay today?" takes any emotional charge out of it. Oftentimes our clients are so relaxed that the last thing on their mind is paying. It is actually a compliment and a sign the work is working!

Rescheduling

At the end of every session, we recommend you have your calendar out. Whether or not you do online scheduling, it is a way of showing care. You are holding the therapeutic container for clients to rebook if that is right for them, rather than saying, "Oh, just go online."

People value that personal connection. Sometimes they want to discuss with you when they should come back. We view that as an opportunity to encourage them to reflect for themselves, and then it will turn into a conversation. That personal interaction helps our clients feel taken care of and nurtured, and it is a prompt for them to assess the benefits they are receiving from our work.

Over time we get to know our clients' preferred way of rebooking. Many will choose to rebook at their session, and some do better when they can check their schedule at home and use our online systems. Kate has a client who always has a couple of sessions booked ahead on the schedule. After each session, once she gets home, she books herself another even farther out. It is a rhythm that works for her, and if there were a change in that, it would be a good time to check in and have a conversation about her needs.

Taking in Gratitude and Acknowledging Your Worth

How we end a session has a powerful impact and it is worth spending time reflecting on how you do this. Part of holding a therapeutic container is how we respond to being thanked. Notice what happens in your body when you are thanked for your work. We all have our habitual ways of responding. It might be, "You really did the work" or, "Oh, you did such good work today," or, "It was my pleasure."

These are all valid replies. Though after some reflection we have noticed that saying, "You're welcome," acknowledges the gratitude and it also acknowledges the value that our clients are expressing toward us and our work. It is one way for us to step up into our worth. "You're welcome" is a clean way to end a session when you have been thanked, whereas the other phrases above may convey some discomfort in receiving gratitude, and also leave more room for conversation. A simple expression of thanks may be all your client is wishing to convey.

Testimonials

A great way to build business is to ask clients for testimonials about their work with us, so we can use them for our marketing. The other thing testimonials do is help us recognize the good work we are doing. For those of us who tend to doubt our work's worth, asking for testimonials can be a game changer.

Writing a testimonial also helps our clients recognize for themselves how valuable the work is. Robyn shares this experience about being asked to write a testimonial:

> I had been taking an online program for my own growth and the leader asked me to write about my experience. I thought the program was valuable, but now I really know just how much I'm getting because I was asked to think about it. I've signed up for the next round because I could spell out for myself how far I've come and what I might like next.

It may seem daunting to ask your clients for testimonials. But it is not complicated, and most people are happy to do it when given a clear request. You can simply approach a client who is happy with their progress, and ask if they would be willing to answer some questions about your work together. Remember that if you would like to quote people, be sure to ask their permission (even if you just plan to use their initials). These questions from Anne Sagendorph-Moon, that we shared with you in Chapter 3, work well for us:

- Why did you come to work with me?
- What did you expect to accomplish?
- How has the work we have done benefitted you?
- What was unexpected or surprising about working with me?
- What one thing would you like people to know about me and my work?

MOVING BEYOND OUR HABITUAL MONEY STORIES

Anne told our classes, "Everybody has a money story. Every human being. I've had people who grew up in wealthy homes and they still had issues about money. I've had people who grew up in true poverty and they have issues about money."

Anne recommends that each of us take the time to write out our money story: our early recollections of how our family dealt with money, and how we think about and relate to money. She has found that for most of us, the emotion that usually sits with money is shame. It is also common to have a constant inner dialogue about money with repeated thoughts like, "Oh, money never shows up for me," or, "Oh, God, I hope I can pay my bills," which underneath is reinforcing the idea, "I'm not going to have the money to pay my bills."

Anne believes that everybody can shift their relationship with money once they are aware of the stories that they continually tell themselves in the background and then do the work to shift their beliefs about money. She cautions us that using positive self talk without uncovering the emotions at play is not effective. Until that inner dialogue changes, she says, it is hard to have money flow easily.

If this is something that you already know is an issue for you, consider seeking support around it. Tapping or EFT (such as Nick Ortner's work: www.thetappingsolution.com) can be very helpful. Another helpful technique that Anne recommends is having a forgiveness and gratitude practice.

In her work with Anne, Robyn created a practice of looking for ways to experience money as delightful (instead of filling her with anxiety), and to be on the lookout for surprises. This can sound small, but it actually was quite meaningful. She would celebrate finding money on the sidewalk, an unexpected discount at the store, or the extra bunch of greens tossed in her bag as a "thank you" from a vendor at the farmers market.

Robyn combined this effort at anticipating delight with a firm commitment to being ahead of all her financial commitments and giving a set percentage of her income to people and causes that she values. She created a new relationship with money, one that felt deeply respectful and loving. This was a complete change from the anxious, resentful attitude around money she had grown up with.

The Benefits of Giving and Receiving

Research shows us that when we give—not just money—but when we give and another person receives, endorphins (our feel-good hormones) are released. This also happens for anybody who is watching the experience! You can give small things or small amounts of money. It is the giving that matters, and the consistency, not the amount. Anne remembers a client who did not have a lot of money when she first started a practice of giving consistently, so she went over to her neighbor's and she put her spare change on the back porch as a surprise. It made her feel abundant and joyful, and that is the point.

Being Ahead of Your Money

Anne teaches her clients to pay their bills before they are due. It is built in to her business as well: she takes payment 10 days before the end of the month for the next month's coaching. She does this because she is a stand for her clients' being ahead of their money, which she has demonstrated helps increase cash flow. You can try this too. Start sending an extra payment toward any debts you have (even if it is just $5 sent between your regular payments). Pay your rent before the first of the month. Pay any (or all!) of your bills before their due date. You are going to have to pay them anyway. Why not send the money in a few days earlier? See for yourself what that does to your own money flow and your experience of money and worth.

We hope that you can see how important the topic of money and worth is in creating a strong Business Container and a strong therapeutic container. This topic really shows us where we have limiting beliefs that hold us back from having a successful therapeutic business. It is often the area that creates the most resistance in us and we would much rather read an anatomy textbook than do this work! If there is one chapter we would recommend you prioritize in sitting down and answering the "Let's Get into Action" questions, it would be this one. Finding a trusted partner to do it with will yield the best results.

Let's Get into Action...

QUESTIONS TO DEVELOP THE MONEY AND WORTH ELEMENTS OF YOUR BUSINESS SUCCESS

- Why do I charge?
- How do I value the work that I do?
- Where am I in my business?
- Am I in a place where I want to be financially? What are the next steps or the next things I want to realize?
- What is my idea of a fair exchange for my work? My experience?
- Take an honest reckoning: do I have a business or a hobby right now? Which do I want?

- How is it for me when I am thanked for my work? Do I confuse gratitude with someone thinking I am the reason for their good results?

- What are my financial needs? Wants? What future expenses do I need to be funding now?

- How will I decide what to charge?

- Will I offer a sliding scale? Do I wish to meet my clients' needs for different fees another way?

- How do I recognize when it is time to raise my rates? How do I decide my new fee, and how will I communicate that?

- What is my system for rebooking clients?

- Do I regularly check in on my clients' sense of progress and satisfaction with the work?

- How do I value my work?

- Which clients would I like to get testimonials from?

- What is my stance on trading?

- Have I considered the biases and stories I have around money?

CHAPTER 6

PROFESSIONALISM, ETHICS, STANDARDS AND SCOPES OF PRACTICE

This book would not be complete without addressing how we develop and maintain ethical and therapeutic standards within our businesses. Many of us start our practices and only begin to address ethical issues as they arise. But when you want to create a full, thriving business it is important to know where you stand on issues that can get thorny. It is vital to get support and put plans in place before you run into troubles.

In our experience, developing clarity in this realm has been key to creating robust Business Containers. Engaging with these topics increases our self-awareness, which is in alignment with our Business Paradigm. Our increased awareness allows us to be more present for our clients. And our referral sources consistently tell us that they value and rely on our high level of professionalism.

We cannot foresee every ethical dilemma we may encounter, but thinking through those we *can* anticipate helps us avoid panic when something unexpected crops up. We already have developed a sense of our own ethical standards and can apply what we have learned to new situations. Knowing where you stand ethically supports you, your business, and your therapeutic field as a whole.

We have divided this chapter loosely into four sections: how we interact with clients, with colleagues, with our professional organizations, and with the government.

HOW WE INTERACT WITH CLIENTS

This section is about how we maintain healthy boundaries in the relationships we have with our clients. We share how we have come to define business boundaries for ourselves. We hope that this provides you with a springboard to create your own clarity. Like other topics in this book, the list is not exhaustive, but is meant to get you thinking.

Being Honest About Skill Level, Licensing, and Certifications

We truly believe that clients can receive benefit from practitioners at all skill levels: ones who are just starting out and those who have decades of experience. It is the fit between client and practitioner that is key. So it does us no good to pretend to have more experience than we actually do (nor does it serve us to sell our years of experience short). Please be honest about where you are in your practice. Clients can tell when we overstate our experience or hedge.

Consider this example: at what point in our practice do we work with populations with special needs or who may require specialized training or skills beyond our core training? In CST, one such population is children. Their bodies are just different enough from adults that a specialized curriculum has been developed for the therapists who work with them.

Some colleagues feel it is sufficient simply to have read the cautions that should be observed when working with young children, but we have each chosen to receive specific pediatric training. There is no rule that prevents therapists who do not have this training from working with children: it is a choice that each therapist has to make, based on their personal and professional sense of ethics. Can you think of an issue like this in your own practice?

These are questions that can help guide you:

- Where is my skill level?
- What is my experience?
- What is my licensure? Does it entitle me to work with this population?

You can then make an informed decision that you can feel comfortable standing behind.

Being Honest About Your Scope of Practice

Developing clarity around your scope of practice strengthens your Business Container and therapeutic container. Kate is a licensed physical therapist and her scope of practice is by definition wider than Robyn's as a massage therapist. We both practice CranioSacral therapy, but Kate has more latitude in other techniques she can employ.

In exploring this topic, think about the recommendations you make to clients. For instance, you might ask yourself if your licensure allows you to diagnose or advise on medication. This area is one that is clearly defined. Working within the boundaries of our professional licensure is vital to the integrity of our business.

You could also take a fresh look at your intake form, which should only include questions that are covered by your scope of practice. It may be tempting to use intake forms from medical practices, since they are widely available. But using a form that asks for information that is out of our scope can give the wrong impression to a client. It also may not give us the information that is most relevant for our work.

Committing to staying within our scope of practice helps us quickly identify when we begin to be out of our depth. That is our cue to make a referral to an appropriate professional, such as a physician or licensed mental health professional.

Unearned Intimacy

In therapeutic work there is an unavoidable power differential. We can aim to minimize it, but the fact is that there is always a certain amount of what one of our mentors called an "unearned intimacy." People share with us much more than we share with them, in the hopes that we can help them.

In addition, there is an intimacy in the conversations that happen. We imagine that most of you will have heard a client say, "I've never told anybody this." Kate recalls being asked by a male client, "Kate, do people fall in love with you?" In exploring the question with him, she found what he meant by that was, "A lot of what we talked about today, I'd only really talk about with my spouse."

Often, clients are sharing something for the first time and they are taking a chance to trust us. This is a healthy process that can promote a healing response in our clients. We may be accustomed to this level of therapeutic connection, but it could be new for our clients. It can be a place where clients get confused because there is deep sharing, and so it is vital that we honor our client's vulnerability by having clarity around our therapeutic role.

Touch Outside Session Work

Our work involves touch, and the boundaries between touch as therapy and touch that conveys more than a therapeutic relationship can be tricky. We need to honor our own boundaries, communicate those clearly and kindly, and above all do our very best not to violate our clients' boundaries.

One common dilemma that we have encountered and heard about from our colleagues is how to approach hugging. It is not uncommon for clients and therapists to share a hug at the end of a session. Do you know where you stand on this issue? The close of a session is still the session, so the work is continuing, and therefore we want any action we take to be centered on the client's well-being.

We think therapists get into trouble ethically when they feel very comfortable initiating a hug to end the session. That brings up the question: who is this contact for, the client or the therapist? Kate had a client who shared with her that he would not continue to see a colleague of hers because she hugged him at the end of the session, and he was not at all comfortable with that. For him, it felt like a violation of his boundaries.

There are certain clients for whom it is a routine at the end of the session. They like to have a hug, and we are more than happy to oblige, but we wait for their initiation. If for any reason you are not comfortable with a hug, you may wish to think about how you will approach that before the situation presents itself. Consider what your physical stance will be and how you will end the session warmly, but without contact.

Sometimes with young children we will have the ritual of a hug at the end of their sessions. One of the reasons we started offering them hugs is that we found once we ended the session and they were out the door, they would run back to have one! It seemed the session was not complete for many of our small children until they had that hug to end it. When we do offer a hug, we kneel down to ask, "Would you like a hug?" A hug with them is always on their grounds, with their permission. It is not assumed. A high five or fancy handshake can work just as well: it is a ritualized form of contact to signal the session has ended since children do not have the ritual of paying and rescheduling.

How We Dress for Sessions

We would perhaps like to think we are not judged by how we look, but we are. Our appearance is often the first impression people have of us. We reflect our profession in how we dress. As bodyworkers, we require clothing that allows us to move comfortably. How do we balance comfort and ease of movement with a professional presentation?

Dressing in a way that you think reflects the status of your work is something to think about, and considering how we wish to present ourselves has certainly helped us. We wear what we call "work clothes," which are different from what we wear around the house or what we would wear out for fun. Our mindset is, "I'm going to work."

When we are dressing for work, we consider distractions such as drapey sleeves that could touch our clients inadvertently. We avoid jewelry that makes noise or that dangles and gets in the way of our contact. And we pay attention to necklines and waistbands. Basically, we decide how much of our body we wish to be seen, and we consider how our clothing moves with us so we do not have to adjust a top that rides up or pants that slide down.

Office Décor and Sensory Issues

Our work space will affect our clients. We often just assume that our workspace is neutral and welcoming. Ideally, clients will feel comfortable enough in our space to relax and do their work, but not so comfortable that they want to stay all day! A good exercise is to walk into your work area as if you were a client. Look around with fresh eyes to see if you are presenting yourself the way you wish to be seen.

Does your office reflect you and your approach to your work? How might a client with different tastes, religious beliefs, or movement capabilities feel in your office? Are there trip hazards? Is the lighting distracting when someone is supine on your table? What do clients see when they sit in the chair you provide them? Is there a designated spot and sufficient room for what they bring with them (purses, backpacks, shoes)?

How is the atmosphere for people with sensory difficulties? Many people are sensitive to scents (even therapeutic essential oils), and some people are very sensitive to electromagnetic influence. You may still choose to diffuse an oil or have Wi-Fi in your office, but make it a choice and be willing to let your clients know that you use these things.

If you display religious items, be aware that they may be triggers for people or make them uncomfortable. You can make your choices a bit more neutral by acknowledging them and saying, "I recognize this is my belief system, and here's my intention for you."

Note Keeping and Recording Sessions

Some professional licenses mandate record keeping and others do not. We recommend that you understand what is required of you by your licensure or certification and be diligent about your record keeping.

Then there are the situations we would not have imagined. At the end of one recent multihands session, a client asked if we would write up for her what had happened during the session. Kate's response to this was:

> Well, that's coming through my filter. If I write something down for you, I'm giving you an impression of the session that's run through my system. I think it would be more beneficial for you if you sat and journaled, because then it's coming through your own system. You're going to deepen your session by doing that. You're going to gain more information that will be meaningful and true to you.

Notice this client was not asking for our session notes, but for us to actually tell her what had happened in the session. We have had clients ask us to write things down for them during a session, and we are perfectly fine with that if they are doing the dictation. We are also familiar with a client sitting up and saying, "Wow! What happened?" Our response, rather than tell them our impression is, "So what struck you?" Again, we are prioritizing our client's experience.

Occasionally we will have a parent ask to video sessions. We have a discussion to clarify what the parent hopes to gain. By having the conversation, we have found that many parents want to understand what is happening in sessions and think video will provide that clarity. We then can actually meet their needs and give them insight and explanations. We may also suggest that the parent's time would be better spent participating in the session or actively observing it. We have no objections if the video is used to help the medical team and other caregivers who are not present, but we do create a brief contract stating that the video is exclusively for that purpose, should always be viewed in its entirety, and not be made public. Knowing the reason behind a request is always helpful.

Nonclients Attending Sessions

Think about the people you are comfortable having in your office while you treat. Knowing this and the behavior you expect—and communicating it to those in the room—will make your sessions run more smoothly.

Here are some questions to consider:

- Are you comfortable having a client's children sit unaccompanied in your waiting room while your client has a session?

- If you work with children, what do you expect from parents or guardians during the session?

- How do you feel about a parent bringing the entire family for one child's session?

- Is it okay for a client to bring a friend to observe a session?

- What expectations do you have about a non-client's behavior during sessions? For example, is playing video games okay? Having conversations that do not have to do with treatment?

Kate recently had a new client ask if she could bring in a friend to observe because the friend is fascinated by CranioSacral therapy. Kate said:

> Absolutely okay on my end, but I would like you to think about how it is for you. Do you feel that this will support you in what will happen? There may be some things that are personal to you that would come up if you were by yourself that may not if your friend is sitting there.

Working with Clients Who Have Guardians Giving Consent

When working with adolescents, the hard rule is that this is a person who is not legally able to take full responsibility for their well-being. The parent or legal guardian is responsible. When it is appropriate to see an older adolescent alone, it is a good idea to have a written release completed to document informed consent from the parent/ guardian.

We both have worked with adult clients who are not able to give informed consent: those in comas, those who have severe developmental disabilities, or those with severe traumatic brain injury. In these cases, we are working at the request of guardians, and it is our policy that the guardians are present for the sessions.

Take some time to consider your own thoughts on:

- When do you ask that a guardian stay in the room?
- If your scope of practice does not explicitly cover this, are there situations where you are comfortable working with a minor without the parent in the room? Do you ask that the guardian stay close by?
- How will information from the session be shared with the guardian?
- How will you get feedback about the sessions from the client and guardian?
- Are you a mandated reporter?
- What action will you take if you become aware of information that poses harm to your client or someone else?

Sharing Personal Information with Clients

Over the years we have had encounters that prompted us to create our own guidelines around how much personal information we are willing to share. The guidelines we follow are based on two rules:

- keeping the focus on our clients and their process
- lowering the power differential whenever possible

Following both of these means that sometimes we will share personal information and sometimes we will not! Context is everything.

We remember a client we worked with together in a multihands session. It was his very first session and he was deep into what we would call a somatoemotional release process. All of a sudden he said, "So where do you live, Robyn?" We just took that as, "Oh, perhaps he needs a little break." So Robyn shared where she lives, and a little later in the session he suddenly asked, "So you didn't grow up in America, Kate. Where did you come from?" Kate's accent gets people's attention. Again, Kate was more than happy to answer. It is not like we gave long answers, just an honoring of his requests, and it was information both of us were happy to share. It was not too personal.

But it was also a choice for us in how we answered. We could have given a slightly clipped or blunt answer, or we may have redirected him to sensations in his body. It can be tempting to judge these questions as inappropriate and sometimes that can be true. However, in this situation (and what we have found to be in true in most situations) it was more about the client feeling safe with us and pacing his own session. When we answered him, we were also paying attention to what was happening therapeutically through our touch. Because he was still deeply in his process, we knew our answers were not derailing his work.

Over time, our clients may wish to know us as people, and it is up to each of us, in every situation, to decide what we want to reveal and what we wish to keep private. It is useful to think about this ahead of time, so when the moment arrives when a client asks, "Do you have children?" or "Who'd you vote for?" you know what you will want to say. When we are at ease with what we are willing to share and what we keep private, our clients will be, too.

Why include this in a book on business? Because it can easily bring up triggers that can catch us off guard. We are exploring issues that can create barriers in our communication in a way that is detrimental to our clients and business. To have a thriving therapeutic business, we need to have explored ethical issues that can engender trust or threaten it. Again, we are presenting topics that require us to do our own self exploration and get support when needed, in keeping with our Business Paradigm.

Confidentiality in the Real World, and Multiple Relationships

People are naturally curious, and we do not think folks have confidentiality in mind when they ask about someone else's session. But we should. When clients ask about each other, or when someone knows another person is a client of ours and wants to know about their session, one of our favorite phrases is, "I imagine you could ask them." We do not try to be too proper or superior about it. It is a gentle way of deflecting rather than saying, "I'm not going to be sharing any information."

There are times when a gentle deflection is not clear enough, so we are also comfortable saying, "I am sorry, but I won't talk about so and so because of client confidentiality. I recommend that you ask them directly." And because it is simply our policy to keep confidentiality, no matter what, there is no emotional content to that statement. It is just a fact. That helps ensure there are no hurt feelings.

As for dual (and multiple) relationships: not only are they possible, sometimes they are unavoidable. Your child's math teacher could become your client. You may work with someone in your book club. You might work with one of your spouse's coworkers. The key is to have healthy, conscious boundaries ahead of time. We like to think of it in terms of membranes: semi-permeable when appropriate, impermeable when needed.

Living in Community with Clients

One of Robyn's teachers taught her that once someone is your client they are always your client, even in the world outside your office after they have stopped seeing you. We both live where we work, so we run into clients and former clients regularly: at the grocery store, the gym, at school pickup, and out on local hiking trails.

We always defer to our clients in how we interact, which means paying close attention to how they are receiving us. Some are excited to see us and want to introduce us to their entire family, some may quietly wave, and some turn and walk the other way. These are, of course, just three examples of a myriad of possibilities. What is important to us is that the client always leads the way.

When clients are with us for some time, they may begin to view us as part of their intimate community. It is not unusual for us to be invited to parties, performances, and life cycle events. We each attend life cycle events for clients with whom we have an ongoing (or have had a significant) relationship.

Robyn has attended religious and graduation celebrations for her pediatric clients, but has chosen not to attend the same life cycle events for the children of her adult clients. We have attended funerals and end-of-life celebrations for our clients, but find that we are most comfortable greeting the family members who know us, sitting in the back, and not overstaying. We pay our respects and go, recognizing that we are members of the care team and not family or close friends. Other therapists do it differently, and we think as long as we each have a considered and conscious decision for why we attend or do not attend, we can be appropriate.

When We Cannot See a Client for Ethical Reasons

What would you do if:

- a seven-year-old client's mother dropped her off early at your closed and locked door and left to pick up another child from school? How would you communicate about this to your client?
- a client you had just seen was later hospitalized after attempting suicide? What support would you need in place to continue seeing them?
- a client starts to use abusive language to you in their communications?
- you do not know why, but you feel uncomfortable with a client and you find that you cannot be grounded in their presence?

Every situation is unique, of course, and as a general rule we recommend transparent communication with all clients. But when we have decided that we can no longer work with a client because of ethical concerns, it may not always be constructive to discuss those concerns with the client. In those very rare cases when communication is not constructive, we simply say, "I think we've gone as far as we can go together with this therapy, and I wish you well." Unless you are mandated by your licensure to provide referrals, there is no need to refer a client who is abusive to you or is not a good fit for the therapy you provide to one of your colleagues.

Transference, Countertransference, and Stepping Outside the Role of Therapist During a Session

This is just a brief introduction to this topic, keeping in mind that we are not mental health professionals. We raise it because these concepts are important for the creation of a healthy Business Container.

Transference is classically defined as a client's/patient's redirecting an experience of emotion that originated in childhood toward their therapist. We prefer to think of it as the unconscious redirection of emotion (from any time of life) toward a therapist or perceived caregiver.

Transference can be used therapeutically by practitioners as long as we are alert, grounded and neutral, and maintain good boundaries. When we become aware that a client is experiencing transference, we can acknowledge the emotion without engaging in the story. It is important to realize that transference is not about us. This realization on our part is most often enough to move a session along productively.

On rare occasions we have had clients who experienced transference repeatedly, with no change in the pattern over several sessions. In those cases, we have felt that it is important to refer the client out and also provide a psychotherapy referral. Perhaps another practitioner will be less triggering of that unresolved emotional pattern and, therefore, will be a better therapeutic match. And if not, a skilled psychotherapist is trained to work directly with these types of issues.

Countertransference is the therapist's transference toward a client. Yes, this happens too! Our job is to be aware of the possibility, remain alert, and get our own work. This makes countertransference less likely to happen, and when it does happen, then we are more likely to be able to recognize it and either correct it in the moment or refer our client out.

Then there are the times that clients ask us for advice or to tell them how we have dealt with an issue in our own lives. We are very aware when we are tempted to take off our practitioner hat/role and have only our human beingness to offer. It is not a situation we find ourselves in often. So we check, double check, and then check again: what are my motives for stepping out of my role as practitioner? Who benefits? And are there particular times/moods/life circumstances for me in which this situation pops up more often?

Answering these questions help us understand if we are truly acting in our client's best interest or if there is self-interest involved. When we do choose to do it, we are transparent about it. "This is my personal experience, and I'm stepping out of my role as therapist here."

Product Recommendations and Retail Sales

For those who regularly use products in the course of our work, and who formulate or recommend products based on our specific expertise, retail sales make sense. Our clients are coming to us for those products and recommendations.

But in a therapeutic business we must remember that our recommendations have more weight with our clients than they would if we were not engaged with them therapeutically. That is why it is ethically tricky to recommend or sell products when it is not specifically within our scope of practice: if we are benefitting from the sale or recommendation, then we may not always have our client's best interest in mind. And our clients may feel a responsibility to buy from us, even if we tell them there is no pressure for them to buy.

Being Mindful of What We Call Ourselves

Do you view yourself as a healer? Do you believe that you are a facilitator and your client does the healing? Or do you have another way of viewing your therapeutic role? It is important to consider the titles we choose for ourselves, because it changes how our clients view both us and themselves.

In keeping with our Business Paradigm, we call ourselves facilitators and avoid any title that implies that we have more power than our clients in the healing process. We encourage you to become clear on the title that you use and the ways you view yourself. Not only will it help you create a more solid Business Container, it will also support you with your marketing material.

HOW WE INTERACT WITH COLLEAGUES

In this section, we are going to be exploring the concept of confidentiality and how we vet referral sources.

Referring to Other Practitioners

Providing good referrals is one of our chief joys in this work. We love to help build a good team for people. Why do we refer to other practitioners? In general, we refer clients to other practitioners when: 1) we are not a good fit or, 2) we feel our client would benefit from a therapy that is outside our scope of practice. In the first case, we are sending the client on their way and do not expect to treat them again. In the other case, we may continue seeing our client or may suggest a break in treatment.

When we refer, we are transparent about our thought process with our clients. Since we actively track the results our clients are getting with our work, we might say something like:

> We've both noticed that while you've had a lot of improvements, this particular issue hasn't shifted since we started working together. I'd like to refer you to Susan, a practitioner I really trust. I think she has the right skills to help you with this piece. How does that sound?

We continue a conversation that empowers our clients, demonstrates that we care about the results that they are getting from our work, and shows we have their best interests in mind.

By and large, we will not refer to other practitioners unless we have paid for a session from them ourselves. That is one way of ensuring that we are referring to people whose work we know to be useful. Sometimes we will recognize the quality of another practitioner's work because a client will have seen them for a period of time and experienced good results. That alone may give us the insight we need to refer our clients.

We always aim to refer clients to practitioners we believe will be a good fit for their unique needs. We each maintain a large list of practitioners to whom we refer, and we tailor our referrals carefully. Because we do not want any motivation other than our client's best interest, we never participate in networks that provide payment for referrals.

Occasionally we will receive a gift from another practitioner to whom we have referred, or who wants us to refer to them. We always send them a thank you note that states, "I think of you for referrals when they are a good fit for a particular client." We also listen carefully to feedback because a practitioner's way of working can shift, and sometimes then we can no longer refer to them in good conscience. If we hear negative feedback about a practitioner from two or three people or over time, we really pay attention to that and adjust accordingly.

When we see clients who are referred by other practitioners, we express our gratitude for those practitioners' trust in us. If a practitioner is someone we share clients with often, we may send a simple text or email that maintains client privacy like, "Thanks for sending EB my way." If the referring practitioner is someone we do not have a close working relationship with, we send a handwritten note expressing thanks for their trust in our work with their clients.

Confidentiality Again!

Some of us deal with insurance and medical records and are bound by HIPAA (the US's "Health Insurance Portability and Accountability Act"). If that applies to you, we encourage you to educate yourself on those rules and create systems within your practice that ensure that you are in compliance. Many of us are not bound by HIPAA, but that does not mean we do not take consistent care of our clients' privacy. The clearer we can be with the terms we use, the less confusion our clients will have and the clearer our work will be.

What we are all bound by is confidentiality. That includes how we do or do not speak with other practitioners about our clients. We do not share client information unless compelled by law. That is not because of HIPAA, but because ethically it is wrong. We keep our clients' information private, and Robyn lets them know that on her intake form: "Unless required to share it by law, the information you share with me is private; it belongs to you."

Sharing information with a client's other providers. There are, however, instances where it would be helpful to share session information with a client's other providers. If we recommend another practitioner and want to be kept current with their treatment, we will get a signed consent at the bottom of our client's intake form. Oftentimes it is the client who says, "I'd really like it if you could talk to my endocrinologist." That is our cue to pull out their intake form and add a line for consent. It can be as simple as, "I give Robyn permission to speak with Dr. Greatskills about my care."

There are some cases where we feel it is necessary to have regular contact with a client's medical team. For instance, when a client has serious mental health issues we may require that they work with a psychotherapist in tandem with our work, and that we share information. We may also request contact with a client's physician, or at least obtain a physician's written permission to perform our therapy when a client has uncontrolled and/or chronic medical issues.

Sharing information with a client's team can be a powerful way to promote your work. When a client tells you that another one of their practitioners has noticed improvement, and your client has talked with them about your work together, you may wish to have a conversation with that practitioner. We have simply asked clients to sign a release: "Would you mind if I contacted your naturopath/chiropractor/acupuncturist to discuss the work we're doing? I'd love to offer them some information on CST."

We then send that practitioner a copy of the release, and write a brief letter offering to provide information: "I'm pleased to hear that you're seeing positive changes in ClientP as the result of our work together. I'd be happy to have a conversation about P's case and XYZ therapy. I'm including information about my therapy and my practice." We are sure to include brochures, some cards and, of course, our contact information.

You could just ask your client to hand your card to her other practitioner, but that puts the onus on your client and their provider. We recommend taking initiative and being of service. It is also a great idea to reach out to the practitioners who are referring clients to you. Not only does it help with increasing referrals, we also find that we usually learn more from a clinical perspective.

Keeping confidentiality when making referrals. When we refer to another colleague, we give our clients clear reasons. "I'm sending you to Kathy because I think her approach is going to blend well with the way that you work. She is lovely and really soft in her approach and has a great presence." We will give detailed reasons to our client, and then we call the therapist to say, "I've sent you a client, first name this. I think you're a good fit," and that is as far as it goes. The client gets information about their new therapist, and we give the bare minimum to the therapist, to protect our client's privacy.

Talking about clients with our colleagues. When we are among fellow therapists and we let our guard down, it is really tempting to talk about our cases when we are talking shop. We participated in a supportive group of therapists where we would share about our cases and found it to be very valuable learning.

But we want to provide some words of caution about sharing information between colleagues. Even though we are sharing among our professional peers and may assume confidentiality applies, we do not always know who knows whom. We do not know what identifying details might tip someone off to the identity of our client. The rule that we guide ourselves by is if what we say were to get back to our client, our client's mother or son, or to someone who was thinking about working with us, would we be completely comfortable with what we have shared?

Have you thought about how you share information with your loved ones or friends, or when writing a social media post about a really interesting session? It is natural to want to share about your day. And unless we have been taught in a program that addresses these issues, it can be easy to think, "What's the harm?" But there is a stark difference between sharing session details in a closed group of colleagues who are all bound by confidentiality, and sharing those same details with one's significant other or in a public forum.

To share outside the bounds of confidentiality, we need explicit permission. So, for instance, we have specific and explicit permission from all the clients whose stories we share in our published articles. The same goes for all the client stories in Kate's book.

Our general rule of thumb, one that applies to many aspects of our businesses, is that we treat our clients the way we like to be treated. It is very important to us that we can trust our therapists not to share our personal details with their friends and family. When we find ourselves needing to process aspects of the work we are doing with one of our clients, we do not speak with our friends and family about it. We seek help from our trusted colleagues and mentors. When we are being interviewed or giving a talk, we change identifying details. We will also combine several client's sessions into one vignette so that we can convey our point without violating anyone's privacy.

In order to have a healthy, thriving business we need to come to a place of clarity and comfort so that our business has nothing holding it back. This demands that we spend time exploring the rules that govern our profession and our own ethical values, and how they impact our policies and behavior. We highly recommend exploring confidentiality issues with a mentor. Many concerns are clear cut, but it can take time and experience to develop a sharp sense of what is above board and what is a breach.

Receiving Mentoring / Supervision

Some of us must have supervision before getting licensed. This is when an experienced practitioner in our field provides guidance and feedback as we hone our clinical skills. We hope that all of us will seek out mentoring and supervision in our businesses as well as our practices—required or not—because it is an excellent way to work on ethical issues.

Not every field has an official mentoring program, but you can always give a more experienced practitioner a call to explore getting individualized help. Our place of training, the Upledger Institute (UI), has set up a mentorship program where trained and certified mentors help practitioners with therapeutic and practice issues. Some have additional skill in business mentoring. We value mentoring so much that we went through the UI's training to become certified ourselves.

We each chose to invest in extensive, structured supervision for both the therapeutic and business aspects of our work. We continue to be mentored regularly, but now it is more informal. We all struggle with ethical questions at some point in our businesses and bringing them to light with a more experienced colleague supports us all professionally.

HOW WE INTERACT WITH OUR PROFESSIONAL ORGANIZATIONS

Belonging to a professional organization provides you with credibility and a profession-specific code of ethics. It helps you stay on top of legislative and scientific developments in your field. Professional organizations may offer insurance for your practice and your business contents, which we recommend you have for security and peace of mind. They also often provide you with resources to market your business such as free websites, free practitioner listings, and written materials to describe what you do.

Many of us will have more than one professional organization: one for our licensure or certification and one for the modality we practice. Kate is a member of American Physical Therapist Association because she is a licensed PT. Robyn is a member of Associated Massage & Bodywork Professionals because of her massage certification. They are also both members of the International Alliance of Healthcare Practitioners (IAHP), the professional organization for Upledger-trained CranioSacral therapy practitioners.

Most professional organizations also offer continuing education that is necessary to maintain licenses and certifications. Even if you are in a field that is not regulated, we highly recommend continuing your education to refine your skills. Most organizations offer ethics trainings. We really enjoy taking these trainings because they are thought provoking and help us maintain our high standards.

For instance, the IAHP offers an ethics class for CST practitioners that Suzanne Scurlock created. It brings a lot of our skills into play. Kate has both her Physical Therapy and CranioSacral therapy codes of ethics printed out at her desk. She values seeing them regularly as a reminder of what standards she is working to maintain. When ethics are presented within the framework of our profession, the scenarios all fit, and we can benefit even more than from a general class.

A Word About Networking Organizations

We know of a number of organizations that promise to build businesses by creating referral networks. We each gave it a try at some point early on, because we had been invited repeatedly over the years. What we realized is that this was not the best way for us to build referrals. It may be terrific for service businesses, but therapeutic businesses require a precise match. Instead, we invested in the process of making appointments with other therapeutic and medical practitioners we thought might good matches for our approach.

That investment in paying for sessions, rather than relying on a business referral network, has paid off: we are both known for giving excellent referrals, and most all the referrals we receive from other practitioners are very good fits for us. It is more time and money up front but becomes very efficient over the long term.

HOW WE INTERACT WITH THE GOVERNMENT

When we talk about the government and governmental agencies, we are talking about keeping good session notes and financial records, paying your taxes, making sure you have a business license (if needed), and maintaining your professional license (if required). Find out what you need to practice your therapy without any need to hide, so you can truly shine your light!

Professional Licensing and Scope of Practice

Licensure is the professional credential that allows you to legally do what you do and to promote yourself. For bodyworkers, it is what allows you to "put hands on." This licensure then guides you in your standards of practice and ethics as well as gives you the legal standing to treat people.

Robyn states that she is a certified massage therapist who is Diplomate-certified in CranioSacral therapy. She does this because there is not a legal designation of "CranioSacral therapist" at this time. We urge you to present yourself in a way that is an honest and true representation of your professional credentials.

It is our licensure (or state-issued certification, in cases like Robyn's) that defines our scope of practice, and at times our scope of practice will be different from the modality we usually perform. When Kate uses her skills in joint mobilization, she will state that to her client. Mostly she is using the skills she learned in her CST training, however she feels that it is important to provide clear communication and promote understanding with her clients. For example, when mobilizing the first rib she will tell the client what she is about to do because of the distinct change in the quality of touch.

Robyn has found that on occasion she is called to perform some of the deep tissue work that she is well trained in. Like Kate, she is transparent about when her touch will be markedly different than that of CST. She is more accurately representing the work if she calls it out with just a brief, "Hey, this is a deep-tissue technique, you'll likely notice a difference in pressure." This supports her client's tolerance for sensation, creates transparency about the work, and builds trust, so we consider it a necessary part of ethical practice.

When There Is No License or Certification for What You Do

Licensing and certification varies for professions from country to country and from state to state. Having a certification from a school is not the same as having a state certification or a license.

If you are in a profession that is not licensed where you practice, we recommend that you get advice about how to practice legally. Some states have provisions that allow you to practice your therapy as long as you provide your clients with a detailed description of your scope of practice. One example of this is California's Senate Bill SB577. Do your research and know where you stand.

Reporting Abuse

Some of us are mandatory (or mandated) reporters, as defined by our professional license. But all of us encounter people who may be vulnerable to abuse, such as children, senior citizens, and people with disabilities. We encourage everyone to recognize signs of neglect and physical, emotional, sexual, and financial abuse, no matter your official designation. Have a plan in place and resources at the ready to report abuse that you witness or suspect, and provide helpful referrals as appropriate. There are websites for Child and Adult Protective Services in each state in the US and most countries.

Taxes

We know practitioners who have refused to open their own businesses because they think taxes will be too complicated. We are happy to let you know that most all of us have very simple businesses, and so our taxes are not very complicated at all. Yes, there are a few more forms for people who own businesses, but do not be intimidated. You may choose to use an accountant to get guidance, but it is also just fine to use simple tax software.

Business Licenses

Are you required to have a business license where you practice? It is not hard to find out: check the website for the city or county in which you practice. A business license is not a professional license; most of us will need to have both. Having a business license is another way of shining our light and not operating in the shadows.

Robyn's first office was in a lovely cottage behind a private home. But it was not a legal office, which meant Robyn couldn't publish her address and couldn't get a business license. While in many ways it was a great space, with good light and a beautiful garden, there was always some degree of hiding: clients were encouraged to come and go quietly without drawing attention to themselves, and everyone who worked there was keenly aware that if the neighbors complained, then they might all be out of an office. Robyn hadn't really been aware of any tension, but once she rented a legal space she felt a burden lift.

We hope that you can see how maintaining ethical boundaries is vital to the success of a therapeutic business, and that you will recognize the value in setting aside time to explore ethical issues that relate to your practice before trouble arises. As we have been saying throughout this book, whatever we leave unexamined regarding our business is where we are likely to falter. Unexamined ethics topics can create a leaky Business Container and lead to a less-than-ideal reputation out in the world. Actively exploring potential ethical issues and addressing them as soon as they come to our awareness is important if we wish to have good standing within our community.

Let's Get into Action...

QUESTIONS TO DEVELOP THE PROFESSIONALISM, ETHICS, STANDARDS AND SCOPES OF PRACTICE ELEMENTS OF YOUR BUSINESS SUCCESS

CLIENTS

- How do I describe my ethical standards in business?
- How do I define my scope of practice?
- How do I speak about my licensure/certification?
- Do I hug at the end of the session? How do I decide?

- How do I dress for work?
- How do I consider décor and other sensory factors?
- What are my record-keeping obligations?
- What are the ways I honor client confidentiality? Are there areas I need to tighten up?

COLLEAGUES

- What is my decision-making process in making referrals?
- How do I honor client confidentiality with colleagues?
- Am I aware of any tricky or challenging situations?
- Would I benefit from mentoring/supervision?

PROFESSIONAL ORGANIZATIONS

- Are there professional organizations that are meaningful for me to be a member of? Why?
- Is there value in belonging to a networking group?

GOVERNMENT

- Am I clear on my scope of practice within in my licensure?
- Do I have a plan in place and resources ready to report abuse?
- Am I clear on my tax obligations? Do I need to seek out support?
- Do I need to have a business license, and how will I obtain it?

ACKNOWLEDGMENTS

A deep bow of gratitude to the following people, without whom this book would never have been written:

Dr. John E. Upledger, who developed the work we are so fortunate to practice, and whose treatment paradigm was the impetus for our approach to business.

The instructors and staff at the Upledger Institute International, whose dedication to Dr. John's therapeutic paradigm has informed us deeply. A special heartfelt thanks to our mentors, whose support has shaped us into the practitioners we are today: Tim Hutton, PhD, LMP, CST-D, Suzanne Scurlock, CMT, CST-D, and Tad Wanveer, LMBT, CST-D.

Our students in the Elements of a Successful CST Business online classes—thank you. We were delighted at how you engaged with our material and impressed by the unique ways you've built your businesses.

Our clients—you inspire us every day with your commitment to living your lives with more health, meaning, and enjoyment. To echo a quote from Dr. John: each one of you is a privilege. And we couldn't do what we do without you: you are the other half of our business success!

Our experts from the online class, who shared their knowledge and gifts so freely: Lauren Doko, Anne Sagendorph-Moon, and Suzanne Scurlock.

Our early readers, who made this book, well, readable. Thank you to Rebecca Goettsche, PhD, who provided key insights at a crucial juncture; Ellen Synakowski, RCST®, MA, who supported us with her keen editor's eye, a deep knowledge of craniosacral work, and who gave us the nudge to write this book; and Staci Copses, MS, OTR/L, CBIS, CST-D, who knows our material inside and out, and helped us with style and consistency.

The village of friends who have supported and nourished us along the way. Cheerleaders are so needed and often underappreciated!

And most importantly, our families, who have patiently supported us through the creative process of writing and editing another book (and have listened to far too much business talk).